MYSTERIOUS CELEBRITY DEATHS: THE INTERVIEWS

MYSTERIOUS CELEBRITY DEATHS: THE INTERVIEWS

Volume 4

ALAN R. WARREN
ERIC SHAPIRO

Copyright

Mysterious Celebrity Deaths: The Interviews
Written by Alan R. Warren
Published by House of Mystery

Copyright @ 2021 by Alan R. Warren

All rights reserved. No part of this book may be reproduced, scanned, or distributed in any printed or electronic form without permission of the author. The unauthorized reproduction of a copyrighted work is illegal. Criminal copyright infringement, including infringement without monetary gain, is investigated by the FBI and is punishable by fines and federal imprisonment. Please do not participate in or encourage privacy of copyrighted materials in violation of the author's rights. Purchase only authorized editions. This is a work of nonfiction. No names have been changed, no characters invented, no events fabricated.

Cover design, formatting, layout, and editing by Evening Sky Publishing Services

Published in United States of America
ISBN (Paperback): 978-1-989980-26-2
ISBN (eBook): 978-1-989980-25-5

CONTENTS

Foreword — vii
Introduction — xi

PART I
Kurt Cobain — 3

1. **What people do for Money** — 12
   Interview with Matthew Richer
2. **Suicide Note** — 55
   Interview with Dr. Carol Chaski

PART II
Marilyn Monroe — 83

3. **Declassified** — 90
   Interview with Paul David
4. **Case Closed** — 129
   Interview with Jay Margolis & Richard Buskin

PART III
Bob Crane Murder — 167

5. **DNA** — 171
   Interview with John Hook
6. **Like father, like son** — 213
   Interview with Robert David Crane

PART IV
Natalie Wood — 239

7. **The Ship's Captain** — 241
   Interview with Marti Rulli
8. **The Hollywood Sister** — 261
   Interview with Lana Wood

PART V
Princess Diana — 281

9. **John Morgan** — 285
   Interview with John Morgan
10. **Alan Power** — 321
    Interview with Alan Power

About Alan R. Warren — 338
About Eric Shapiro — 340
Also in the House of Mystery Radio Show Interview Series — 342

Foreword

BY ERIC SHAPIRO

Alan R. Warren is a lunatic.

No, I'm serious. Al is completely unhinged. I co-host with him on his *House of Mystery Radio Show*, and I spend most of each episode marveling over his unique qualities of mind.

This book bears out what I have said above: lunatic, unhinged. It's been culled from his on-air interviews with experts on or studiers of the deaths of Kurt Cobain, Marilyn Monroe, Bob Crane, Natalie Wood, and Princess Diana.

As Al explains in his forthcoming Intro, for each of these celebrity's deaths, there's an official version and an unofficial version. There's the approved media version and the "unknown" alternative version. There's what people think they know and what people (according to Al's guests) would probably be better off knowing. And as Al navigates these choppy waters, he does so with a staggering degree of level-headed sobriety and open-eared curiosity.

He has no horse in the race. In other words, he's not bringing his gavel down on any side of the argument. He's not even so much as *hinting* as to where he might stand. My opinion? He doesn't stand anywhere. Behind his calm poker face is a calm poker mind (and I'll let Al have the fun with puns relating to "poker" … OK, just one! → *Poke her?! I hardly know her!*)

When I say, "He doesn't stand anywhere," I don't mean to say that he's a "Nowhere Man," devoid of any meaningful point-of-view. No, I'm saying he's a "Somewhere Man," and that "somewhere" happens to be the Land of Reason.

That's why Alan R. Warren is insane.

In a media landscape so littered with noise and in a public "conversation" so overcome with shrillness, he actually has the (open) nerve to go at potentially outrageous topics with a tranquil and receptive mind. Like every good host, he listens. Like every great host, he asks incisive questions. And like every exceptional host, he gets the guest's perspective flowing like white-hot lava (again, I'll leave the puns to Al).

In the end, what you get is food for thought. I like that. Being encouraged to think goes down much easier (Al? Pun!) than being told what to think. The latter's religion. The former's science. The latter is fanaticism. The former is basic intellect.

Imagine a world so intellectually impoverished, so thoroughly devoid of rational perspective or analysis, that it takes a total madman to bring balance and clarity back into the equation.

Actually, you don't have to imagine that world because you're already living in it.

But fortunately, Al R. Warren is, too. And he's here to lead you down a deep, dark rabbit hole (uh-huh) toward ideas and theories that could wreck simpler minds. But in Al's hands, minds do not get wrecked. They get opened.

Come on down.

Introduction

The *House of Mystery Radio Show* has been on the air for ten years now, broadcasting in over a dozen cities in the United States, including KKNW 1150 A.M. Seattle/Tacoma, KCAA 106.5 F.M. Los Angeles/102.3 F.M. Riverside/1050 A.M. Palm Springs. I started the show to find out as much information on the world's mysteries in areas of Crime, Science, Religion, history, paranormal, and more. Like most people, I have heard stories, rumors, and read books or watched documentaries on television, but would seldom hear one direct answer to a question.

Throughout my time recording interviews, I sought out people who had themselves researched a subject enough to have written a book or created a documentary, or even people involved in the event or topic that would have first-hand knowledge.

In most cases, the strange thing was that there was a popular or mainstream idea about what happened, one reported at the time of the event, but then there was an alternative idea. Most writers who had books or shows that did well quite often disagreed with the current theory and would accuse the media of faking the story and hiding the truth from everyone.

An example would be "Who shot JFK?" There has been a well-known theory reported by different government agencies and news media that most people in America have come to accept as the truth. But since the original Warren Report on JFK's assassination, there have been hundreds of theories promoted by many authors and lots of research completed.

In this series, we review the most accepted explanation on the topic. Then, we follow up with each of the alternative theories presented during our interviews with the person or people reporting them. There will be no committed answer at the end of the book. Our goal is to provide a concise review of the extraordinary things we learned during the show's interviews.

Each book in this series lays out the topic's details and then follows up with what we've learned from each guest. This book, like the others in the House of Mystery Radio Show Interviews Series, does not attempt to solve the case but only review it. It is an excellent reference for researchers and a good overview for people who don't know the topic well. Similar to the other volumes in this series, only the highlights of each interview will be included.

All of these interviews, and more, are available to listen to on my website: *alanrwarren.com/hom-podcast-episodes*

Volume 4 of the Interview Series, "Mysterious Celebrity Deaths," covers interviews relating to the mysterious deaths of the influential rock band Nirvana's frontman Kurt Cobain, the 1960s mega-icon Marilyn Monroe, TV's *Hogan's Heroes* lead actor Bob Crane, the talented and multi-award-winning actress Natalie Wood, and the people's princess, Princess Diana.

PART I
Kurt Cobain

Kurt Cobain was the lead singer and guitarist of the American rock band Nirvana, one of the most influential acts of the 1990s and one of the bestselling bands of all time. Cobain suffered from chronic bronchitis and intense pain throughout most of his life due to an undiagnosed chronic stomach condition. He was also prone to alcoholism, suffered from depression, and regularly used drugs and inhalants. Two uncles of his cousin had killed themselves using guns.

On March 3, 1994, Cobain was hospitalized in Rome following an overdose of painkillers. His management agency, Gold Mountain Records, said that the overdose was accidental and that he was suffering from influenza and fatigue. However, Cobain's wife, Courtney Love, later said the overdose had been a suicide attempt: "He took 50 pills. He probably forgot how many he took. But there was a definite suicidal urge, to be gobbling and gobbling and gobbling."

Cobain mentioned that he had stomach pain so severe during Nirvana's 1991 European tour that he became suicidal and stated that taking heroin. saying it was "the only thing that's saving me from shooting myself right now." Cobain's cousin Beverly, a nurse, said that the family had a history of suicide and that Cobain had been diagnosed with attention-deficit hyperactivity disorder and bipolar disorder.

In Charles Cross's biography, *Heavier Than Heaven,* Nirvana bassist Krist Novoselic is quoted about seeing Cobain in the days before his intervention: "He was really quiet. He was just estranged from all of his relationships. He wasn't connecting with anybody." Novoselic's offer to buy dinner for Cobain resulted in unintentionally driving him to score heroin: "His dealer was right there. He wanted to get fucked up into oblivion. He wanted to die. That's what he wanted to do."

Death

On March 31, 1994, Cobain left the rehabilitation center he had checked into the day before, Exodus Recovery Center, by scaling a six-foot brick wall. On April 2, 1994, a taxi driver drove Cobain to a Seattle gun shop, where Cobain received a receipt for firearm shells. Cobain told the driver he wanted to buy shells because he had been burglarized.

On April 8, 1994, Cobain's body was discovered in the greenhouse above the garage at Cobain's Lake Washington Boulevard East house by VECA Electric employee Gary T. Smith, who arrived that morning to install security lighting. Smith thought he was asleep until he saw blood oozing from Cobain's ear. He also found a suicide note with a pen stuck through it inside a flowerpot. A Remington Model 20-gauge shotgun purchased for Cobain by his friend musician Dylan Carlson was found on Cobain's chest. Carlson had legally purchased it at Stan Baker's Gun Shop in Seattle.

Cobain did not want the gun purchased in his name because he thought the police might seize it for his own protection. The police had taken away his guns twice in the previous ten months. The King County Medical Examiner noted puncture wounds on the inside of both the right and left elbows. The shotgun, a 20-gauge Remington Model 11, was not checked for fingerprints until May 6, 1994. According to the Fingerprint Analysis Report, four latent prints were lifted, but they were not usable. The Seattle police report states that the shotgun was inverted on Cobain's chest with his left hand wrapped around the barrel.

On April 14, 1994, the *Seattle Post-Intelligencer* reported that Cobain was "high on heroin when he pulled the trigger." The paper reported that the toxicological tests determined the level of morphine in Cobain's bloodstream was 1.52 milligrams per liter and that there was also evidence of valium in his blood. The report contained a quote from Randall Baselt of the Chemical Toxicological Institute, stating that Cobain's heroin level was at "a high concentration, by any account." He also stated that the strength of that dose would depend on many factors, including how habituated Cobain was to the drug.

In March 2014, the Seattle Police Department developed four rolls of film that had been left in an evidence vault. According to the Seattle police, the photographs depict the scene of Cobain's corpse more clearly than previous Polaroid images taken by the police. Detective Mike Ciesynski, a cold case investigator, was asked to look at the film because "it is 20 years later and it's a high media case." Ciesynski stated that the official cause of Cobain's death remains suicide and that the images would not be released to the public, but in 2016, the images were released. According to a spokesperson for the Seattle police, the department receives at least one request weekly, mostly through Twitter, to reopen the investigation. This resulted in the maintenance of the basic incident report on file.[1]

Seattle

In 1989, I was wandering around Vancouver, lost in work and surrounded by many people that seemed like being at a busy party, yet very alone. I took a day trip to Seattle with some others I was working with at the time, and I fell in love with the city. Within one year, I lived in an apartment and already worked at a tavern on Capitol Hill called Changes.

Changes had recently gone through some changes, from a Gay pub-like atmosphere, where people would come to play darts or pool and have a beer, to a straight, live band rock club. The grunge scene had really started to take off in the city, and most of the bands that played there were in the category of music.

So, the change in my life that I wanted was here now, finally, working as a bartender in a grunge rock bar by night and in University for music during the day. I instantly connected to everyone, from the people I worked with to the cashiers at the local Fred Meyer store.

Everyone there shared the dreams of the new energy that was going to take Seattle by storm and the world. Bands like Nirvana, Sweetwater, Alice in Chains, Pearl Jam, and more who had mesmerized the pacific northwest for a few years now, was beginning to catch on in California. Looking back, I didn't know that I was in the middle of the change that would be led by my generation. It was built on the sixties' rock and roll, mixed with the punk, new wave of the eighties.

In the eighties, the sixties music and lifestyles had a big influence on us all. It felt real, and they had made a change in the world without knowing that's what they were doing. Now it was about to happen again.

Capitol Hill in Seattle was turning into a cool part of town, located about a twenty-minute walk from the downtown and a cheap place to find an apartment. It had several used bookstores, coffee shops, and clubs. It was becoming known as the safe part of town for gay and alternative-lifestyle people to go. It felt like a family. It seemed we all knew each other, but like all families, it comes with the emotions of jealousy, guilt, love, and hate.

It's funny to remember the times where I worked until 2 or 3 a.m., went and had food and coffee before going home to bed, then getting up and going up to Broadway Street for yet more coffee to start my day. There I would see hungover band members doing the same, and even without knowing their names, I could sit at a table outside one of many coffee shops or stands and just talk.

This brings me to one of the now-famous people I would meet, that I didn't know then, but she would be one of many soon-to-be celebrities. I never saw her play live in the bar I worked at, but she had spent plenty of nights there. "Hey," I said to her as I sat in the same group of tables that she was at. "Oh, hey," was her couldn't-be-bothered-with-me response. The indifference was common for her, as I had seen it before. She was quite down in the mornings, at least every time I ran into her.

Two other men were sitting there and another woman who used to book these bands into the clubs and taverns. I ended up getting to know her very well over the years, and it was the reason for me to stop and talk, plus feeling really tired and needing to sit. We would talk about the bands that played last night where I worked or the problems she would be having getting the bands to perform without starting fights with the bar owners.

Then out of nowhere, Courtney jumped from her seat hard enough to knock the metal chair she was sitting on backward to the ground. "You fucking asshole, fuck!" she screamed as she crossed Broadway in between the morning rush of traffic. "Where the fuck did you go last night, cunt!" she continued yelling until she made it to the sidewalk across the street that had a group of about seven people walking together. She crashed into them like she was at a mosh pit during a concert. From there, you could hear a lot of yelling and laughing but could not really decipher what was being said.

I went on about my business talking with the agent, just as everyone else did on the street that morning. Though it was still something that I was trying to get used to about my new life, these sorts of things happened frequently there, and nobody paid much attention to it.

---

1. Suicide of Kurt Cobain - Wikipedia. https://en.wikipedia.org/wiki/Suicide_of_Kurt_Cobain

What people do for Money
INTERVIEW WITH MATTHEW RICHER

In 2016, Mathew Richer and Tom Grant published the book titled, *The Mysterious Death of Kurt Cobain: Suicide or Murder, You Decide*. It was primarily based on Tom Grant's information from when he was hired by Courtney Love, according to him, to find out who had stolen and was using Cobain's credit card. It made no sense, as Courtney was said to have canceled all of his credit cards. This would be the first lie I found during the investigation process with Tom Grant.

The book was wildly popular at the time, and the primary author, Matthew Richer, who wrote the book using Grant's information, was on the book promo tour, so I snagged him for the interview a couple of months after the book's release in the summer of 2016.

Q. What made you write a book about Kurt Cobain and his death?

A. Well, there were a few books out on it, but they were not very good. They had a number of significant errors, and they chased a few false theories. Every time the story got covered, it seemed one step forward and one step backward. I met Tom and convinced him that we should write a book together. So, Tom was the investigator, and I was the author who was going to write the book based on Tom's investigation. Tom still has a lot of evidence, and he took very good notes. He recorded a lot of the conversations he had with people involved in this case at the time. During the research for this book, we discovered a lot of new evidence.

Q. Was Tom's evidence matching up to what you originally thought happened to Cobain?

A. When I found out everything Tom had, I realized that his case was even stronger than I originally believed. When I dug into the case myself, I talked to members of the Seattle Police Department. In this book, we have some of the recorded conversations with members of the Seattle Police Department that are very revealing, and we don't use any anonymous sources in the book. So, I was able to come up with a lot of new information, which really strengthened the case of the murder.

Tom Grant was a private investigator hired by Love to find Cobain after he departed from drug rehab. He has said he believes that Cobain was murdered. Grant's theory has been analyzed and questioned by several books, television shows, films, and the 2015 docudrama, *Soaked in Bleach*.

Grant was still under Love's employment when the body was found. Grant has stated that the events surrounding the death of Cobain are "filled with lies, contradictions in logic, and countless inconsistencies. Motivated by profit over truth as well as a web of business deals and personal career considerations, Courtney Love, her lawyers, and many of Love's industry supporters have engaged to keep the public from learning the real facts of this case."

There are several components to Grant's theory. Grant argues that Cobain could not have injected himself with such a dose and still pull the trigger. Grant does not believe that Cobain was killed by the heroin dose. He suggests that the heroin was used to incapacitate Cobain before the perpetrator administered the final shotgun blast. Grant, Wallace, and Halperin have used the dosage reported in the *Seattle Post-Intelligencer*, not the actual autopsy report, and may not have the correct figure. The Seattle police cannot release the information to the media because reports and records of autopsies are confidential and protected under state and federal law.

While working for Love, Grant was given access to Cobain's suicide note, and he used her fax machine to make a photocopy, which has since been widely distributed. After studying the notes, Grant believed that it was actually a letter written by Cobain announcing his intent to leave Love, Seattle, and the music business. Grant asserts that the lines at the very bottom of the note, separate from the rest, are the only parts implying suicide. While the official report on Cobain's death concluded that Cobain wrote the note, Grant claims that the official report does not distinguish these final lines from the rest of the note and assumes it was entirely written by Cobain.

Despite consulting with many handwriting experts, some disagree with Grant's claims. After spending two weeks examining the original copy, document examiner Janis Parker concluded that Cobain wrote the note. When *Dateline NBC* sent a copy of the note to four different handwriting experts, one concluded that the entire note was in Cobain's hand, while the other three said the sample was inconclusive. One expert contacted by the television series *Unsolved Mysteries* and expressed the difficulty in drawing a conclusion, given that the note being studied was a photocopy rather than the original. But in the same documentary, two other experts found the writing, especially the last four lines, suspicious.

Grant also cites circumstantial evidence from the official report. For example, the report claimed that the greenhouse doors could not have been locked from the outside, meaning that Cobain would have had to lock them himself. Grant said that when he saw the doors for himself, he found that they could be locked and pulled shut.

He also questions the lack of fingerprint evidence connecting Cobain to key evidence, including the shotgun. Grant notes that the official report said Cobain's fingerprints were also absent from the suicide note as well as the pen that had been shoved through it, and yet Cobain was found without gloves on.

None of the circumstantial evidence directly points to murder, but Grant has said he believes it supports the larger case.

In studying the Rome incident, journalists Ian Halperin and Max Wallace contacted Dr. Osvaldo Galletta, who treated Cobain after the incident. Galletta contested the claim that the Rome overdose was a suicide attempt, telling Halperin and Wallace, "We can usually tell a suicide attempt. This didn't look like one to me." Galletta also specifically denied Love's claim that 50 Rohypnol pills were removed from Cobain's stomach. However, they also stated, "Grant believes Courtney may have mixed a large number of pills into Kurt's champagne so that when he took a drink, he was actually unknowingly ingesting large amounts of the drug, enough to kill him. But if that's the case, why did she call the police when she found him unconscious on the floor? If she wanted Kurt dead, why didn't she just leave him on the floor until he died?"

Grant believes that the claim of the Rome incident being a suicide attempt was not made until after Cobain's death. He claims that people close to Cobain, including Gold Mountain Records, specifically denied the characterization prior to Cobain's death. Grant believes that if Rome had truly been a suicide attempt, Cobain's friends and family would have been told so that they could have watched over him.

Others have asserted that the claims by Gold Mountain and others were simply efforts to mask what was happening behind the scenes. Lee Ranaldo, the guitarist for Sonic Youth, told *Rolling Stone*, "Rome was only the latest installment of keeping a semblance of normalcy for the outside world."

Grant spoke to Love's attorney, Rosemary Carroll, at her office on April 13, 1994. He said she pressed him to investigate Cobain's death and that Cobain was not suicidal. Carroll also claims that Cobain had asked her to draw up a will excluding Love because he was planning to file for divorce. Grant said this was the motive for Cobain's death, thus alleging Courtney Love had murdered him.

Carroll also provided Grant with a handwriting practice note that she found in Love's backpack that was left at her home. It has been suggested that the handwriting on this practice note is markedly similar to the handwriting found on the last four lines of Cobain's suicide note.

Grant has contended that another motive for Love wanting Cobain dead was him turning down nearly $10 million to headline the 1994 Lollapalooza festival.

Grant counters the claim that the profits from the sale of casebook kits on his website by stating that it offsets some of the costs of his investigation. Grant stated: "I wrestled with that … but if I go broke, I'll have to give up my pursuit, and Courtney wins."

Sergeant Donald Cameron, one of the homicide detectives involved in the case, specifically dismissed Grant's theory, claiming, "Grant hasn't shown us a shred of proof that this was anything other than suicide." Grant, in turn, has accused Cameron of being a personal friend of Love's. Dylan Carlson told Halperin and Wallace that he also did not believe that the theory was legitimate, and in an interview with Broomfield, implied that if he believed that his friend was murdered, he would have dealt with it himself. In *Kurt & Courtney*, he specifically states that he would kill Love and any others involved if he believed that they had murdered Cobain.[1]

Q. Your book does not have a very good commentary on the Seattle Police Department. Did you get any reaction from them after this book came out?

A. Well, not very good. They're like a lot of institutions. They are very protective of themselves. It is interesting the argument that Kurt Cobain committed suicide is basically the argument from authorities. It's really the only argument the Seattle Police

Department has made. In other words, we're the experts, and we have determined this is a suicide and case closed. That's pretty much all they have said.

Real arguments, of course, rely on evidence. If they had evidence to back this up, they would cite the evidence, but they don't do that. The Seattle media has not been very interested in this case, and I'm not sure why that is. I did reach out to the current Seattle Police Chief, Kathleen O' Toole, who I had met a few times regarding the case. I had known her as we both went to Boston College and we have a lot of friends in common. She is aware of the book, and she did say that she would have one of her detectives read it, but I don't know where it has gone from there.

Kathleen M. O'Toole is an American law enforcement officer who served as Chief of the Seattle Police Department from June 23, 2014, to December 31, 2017. She was previously the first female Commissioner of the Boston Police

Department when appointed by Mayor of Boston Thomas M. Menino in February 2004.[2]

She was hired because the Seattle Police Department has had so many problems with corruption and ineptitude. That's why she was brought in. Now they ruled the case suicide. It's very clear from their own reports from that day, April 8, 1994, at the crime scene, and did not bother to investigate.

Kurt Cobain's body was discovered on April 8th, and the death certificate was signed by the King County Medical Examiner on the following day, Saturday, April 9th. So, they pretty much ruled the case a suicide at the scene that day despite some really glaring evidence.

No interviews were conducted. No victimology. No one interviewed Kurt Cobain's wife, Courtney Love. No one interviewed any friends of Kurt Cobain. Nothing like that was done. It was simply declared a suicide that day by the Medical

Examiner as well as the police department.

Q. Why would they do that? Were they trying to protect Courtney? Did they just not care? What was the reason?

A. I think they were sloppy. I also think that they just did not care. Back then, in the early 90s, you had a lot of these grunge rock stars appear in Seattle. They became very wealthy. They became very influential. And they became a symbol of the city almost overnight. There was a lot of resentment from longtime residents of Seattle from the political establishment towards these people. These people were into heroin, and they dressed like slobs. A lot of people thought it was a bad image for the city.

So, with Kurt Cobain, a lot of people in Seattle simply didn't care. So, it was just a mop-up. We describe this in the book where a former police officer from Seattle talked to Tom Grant, and he said, "What do you care, Tom? Those people are just a bunch of junkies, and it doesn't matter." That was pretty much the attitude that Tom Grant was encountering at that time.

For example, Kurt Cobain's body was released to the funeral home the day after it was discovered and weeks before the toxicology reports were in. Only six days later, he was cremated. When the body is cremated, the case is closed.

In the case of Kurt Cobain, after the body was cremated and Tom Grant started raising some questions to the detective in charge of the case, Sergeant Don Cameron had a kind of "show" investigation after the cremation. The suicide note wasn't analyzed until April 22nd. In May, they decided the check the shotgun and shotgun shells for fingerprints. All this was done after the fact. And just for show because Tom Grant was asking questions.

Don Cameron spent nearly four decades with the Seattle Police Department. Cameron investigated some of the city's most notorious deaths. Ted Bundy, Kurt Cobain's suicide, and earned the respect of many on the force. Cameron joined the department in 1960, moving nine years later to the homicide unit, where he investigated more than 1,000 cases and worked for 11 police chiefs. Cameron retired in 1999 amid a cloud of scandal. An internal investigation alleged that Cameron, who supervised the homicide unit at the time, had failed to report one of his officers for stealing money from a crime scene. Prosecutors later said Cameron helped bury the crime by putting the money back, staging a fake "discovery" of it, and writing a false report.[3]

> The shotgun, for example, was nearly 4 feet long, and it had a large surface over it, one to which someone could leave prints. It had been handled by at least three people before Kurt Cobain had died. There were no fingerprints found on that shotgun, which is unusual because it is a very big weapon, and that suggests that the shotgun had been wiped down. Now, if they had tested the shotgun before they had closed the

case, maybe they could have acted differently. But once police officers close a case, they don't like to be told they made a mistake, especially from a private investigator from Beverly Hills. Police officers have big egos. That's not a secret. And when Tom started pointing out discrepancies in the verdict, they started digging their heels in and have been digging them in ever since.

Q. Is it true that the autopsy report was never released to the public.

A. No, to this day, it has not been released to the public.

Q. Is that standard practice?

A. No, just in the state of Washington. Because autopsy reports are considered private medical records in the state of Washington, so only the next of kin can release that report. So, Courtney Love could order the release of that report if she wanted to, but she's not about to do that.

Q. But the police have access to it, correct?

A. The police have access to it, but they can't make it public. However, some of the toxicology report did leak to the press after the body was discovered. According to the *Seattle Post-Intelligencer,* and later confirmed by the Seattle Police Department, Kurt Cobain had 1.52 milligrams of heroin in his system when he died. Now, 1.52 milligrams postmortem is more than three times the lethal dose of heroin. He would have had to inject a minimum of 225 milligrams of heroin into his veins before he died.

This was a guy who was only 5 foot 7 inches and 120 pounds. So, if he took an enormous dose of heroin, he should have been found with a needle still stuck in his arm. This level of heroin would have incapacitated him within seconds. But instead, we're told that Kurt Cobain was found with two separate injection points, and this has been confirmed. According to Mike Ciesynski of the Seattle Police Department, Cobain was found with two separate injection points, one on each elbow.

So, he injected himself twice, and he replaced the safety tips on the syringes. Instead of passing out with the needle still in his arm as he should have, he replaced the safety tips and neatly put away the drug kit, rolled down his sleeve, then picked up a 4-foot-long shotgun. Even though he was not a big guy and did not have long arms, he picked up this 4-foot-long shotgun and stuck it in his mouth, and pulled the trigger.

Now, that is virtually impossible to do. We talked to several medical examiners, and they cannot figure out how this could have possibly happened. He should have been incapacitated within seconds. There's also the problem of the nature of heroin. There are virtually no cases of someone injecting heroin just before committing a violent act of suicide. We can't find a single case of this ever happening before.

When someone injects heroin, they experience something called the "Rush."

It's this intense euphoria that happens within several seconds of the injection. It lasts for several minutes. Addicts describe it like a sexual orgasm that filters throughout the entire body. That is the experience that people like Kurt Cobain were addicted to.

So, we're supposed to believe that he injected this heroin, and just before this "rush" begins, before it commences, he picks up a shotgun, puts it into his mouth, and pulls the trigger. There's a major contradiction there. That's a question that the medical examiner never bothered to ask, and the Seattle police never bothered to ask.

Mike Ciesynski retired from the Seattle police department in 2017 after serving 37 years. Mike was assigned to the homicide unit for 22 years, 12 of which were in the cold case unit, and is now retired.[4]

Q. Do you believe that someone else injected the heroin into him?

A. Police have to prove murder. They don't really have to prove suicide. That's the danger of a suicide investigation. You have to prove murder to a District Attorney, a court, or a jury. But to prove suicide, you don't really have to do any of that. The police don't have to prove suicide. They can just scribble suicide on the cause of death and move on.

Now, a murder that is staged to look like a suicide, almost any wound that one experiences in suicide can be replicated in a murder. We think Kurt Cobain probably knew the people who were in the room when he died. He agreed to do heroin with them, and at some point, he was injected with more heroin than what he wanted injected with.

Once this enormous amount of heroin put him out cold, someone simply inserted a shotgun into his mouth and pulled the trigger. Another reason why this theory holds a lot of weight is the shotgun used to kill Kurt Cobain was a home defense shotgun – a Remington 20 gauge. The purpose of the shotgun is to really scare off intruders. If you shot it into the wall in a room, it wouldn't penetrate the wall and hit someone in the next room.

This shotgun has an ejection port on the right side of the shotgun. The shotgun was found in Kurt Cobain's hands inverted lying across his chest. So, the ejection port was facing Kurt Cobain's right. However, the spent shotgun shell used to kill Kurt Cobain was found lying on Kurt Cobain's left.

There's no way that shotgun shell could have ejected from that ejection port and landed on his left. The police missed that detail because they were all assuming it was a suicide and just overlooked it. They did record it in their report, however.

Q. Now you believe that Courtney Love, Kurt's wife, was behind his murder?

A. We believe she was behind it. She wasn't there when he died. But we believe she was behind it. And she certainly benefitted from it.

Q. So, you think the money was the main reason? Your book also talks about their constant fighting, a possible divorce, and who would get custody of their child.

A. Well, the primary reason was, we give Courtney Love a biography in the book. And we discuss her as a sociopath, which is what her own mother believes, her grandmother believes, and her friends and relatives certainly believe. A sociopath is someone that has no human conscience at all. They have no feelings of genuine affection or guilt towards anything they do. They have no affection for any human beings. They have no empathy for other human beings or animals. Courtney Love was like this since she was a toddler. She was committed to a mental health treatment center when she was a teenager. She was sent to reform school when she was a teenager. She has quite a history of violence and drugs since she was a little girl.

Her lifelong goal was to be a rockstar. But she didn't have any talent, and she didn't have the looks to be a rockstar either. So, when she married Kurt Cobain because she believed he was going places and he could be a useful springboard for her to become a rockstar. However, she had an album coming out that Kurt Cobain wrote and composed called *Live Through This*. It was coming out in April of 1994, but it was going to be accompanied by at least two very devastating revelations.

One, Nirvana was breaking up, and a big reason they were breaking up was because of Courtney Love. No one in the band could stand her. Kurt Cobain was divorcing Courtney Love. He had asked his attorney, Rosemary Carroll, to hire a divorce attorney. He also asked Rosemary Carroll to have his will changed so that Courtney would not receive any money.

Another reason was probably going to be that when her album came out, it was going to be accompanied by those revelations and possibly the revelation that she didn't write the album herself. So, there was a lot on the line in April. She needed his money. She needed that association with him in order to have success, and she was about to lose it all. She was on the verge of 30, too, which is very old for an aspiring female rockstar.

Courtney had acquired complete control over Kurt Cobain's finances. She took private jets, limousines, and she lived very large. She had all his money, and she had control over all of it. She was not about to give that up. They had a prenuptial agreement that Kurt's management made him sign, so if Kurt were to divorce her, she would not only lose her career, but she was also not going to get any money. Money is the oldest motive in the book.

Q. Have you got a response from Courtney on your theories?

A. Courtney threatened to sue Tom initially when he first started to speak out. Tom's detractors call him a conspiracy theorist. But usually, conspiracy theorists are not part of the case. They talk about it from outside of the case. Tom Grant was there. He was in the middle of the events. He was hired by Courtney Love just days before Kurt's body was discovered.

Tom struggled with blowing the whistle. He wanted to be 100 percent sure that Cobain was murdered. What happened was Courtney started to really change her story. If you listen to some of the recordings (between Tom Grant and Courtney Love), Tom starts to become more confrontational with Courtney, and she becomes increasingly fearful.

In November, *Rolling Stone* magazine published an interview with Courtney where she claimed that Kurt had written her a third suicide note in which he talked about his desire for death. Tom had never seen this suicide note. He had never heard of this suicide note, and Courtney had never shown it to anybody, including the Seattle police. So, Tom knew that she was lying then, and he decided to speak out publicly about what he had learned.

Q. What about his previous attempt to commit suicide? You suggest that it was not real.

A. It was not.

Q. So you think it was done to set this up or PR?

A. Right. I call it framing the narrative. You have to remember now that the press in 1994 wasn't much of an online media. The press moved much slower then. There wasn't much of an alternative media. There really wasn't any alternative media to speak of. You had to rely on the mainstream print media and television, and it was very easy for her to manipulate it. She did this before Kurt Cobain was killed and after.

We describe this in the alleged Rome overdose. In March of 1994, Kurt called his attorney, Rosemary Carroll, and we know this because Rosemary discussed it at length with Tom from Germany. From

Germany, he called Courtney and Rosemary and demanded a divorce. When Courtney flew a few days later with the baby to meet Kurt in Rome, they had already agreed to get a divorce. Kurt had met with her in a hotel room and written a note. A three-page note that's referred to as "the Rome note" describing the reasons that he wanted a divorce. One of them being her ongoing affair with Billy Corgan. The next day Cobain was rushed to the hospital.

According to Courtney, she woke up at 3:30 in the morning and discovered Kurt. She's told different versions of what happened, but she found him overdosed. She waited three hours to call the ambulance. Now, at that time, she believed that Kurt was dead. She called David Geffen at his office from her hotel room and told him that Kurt had committed suicide. She told him that Kurt was continually suicidal, and he had finally gone through with it. That's pretty much the talking point that she has stuck to, and she was the only person who ever believed that.

David Geffen called Nirvana's manager, Donald Goldberg, and told him what Courtney had said. Goldberg did a little research, and he called Geffen back and told him that the phone call was a hoax. Now that's very hard to believe. I think it is very difficult to get David Geffen on the phone. I wouldn't know how to do it. So, we believe that Geffen was right. Courtney really did call him and had that conversation with him that Kurt Cobain really did try to commit suicide.

Kurt Cobain was, in fact, in a 20-hour coma, but he did come out of that coma, and he did survive. At the time, everyone involved, including the doctors, said that it was an accidental overdose. But, what he overdosed on was a mixture of champagne and Rohypnol. Rohypnol is known as the date rape drug. The Rohypnol prescription actually belonged to Courtney. It did not belong to Kurt. So, we believe that Courtney slipped him some Rohypnol in champagne in Rome, and that was the first attempt on his life. But he survived it.

When he returned, he had probably blacked out about the entire thing that happened. But he did not forget his attempt to divorce Courtney. He told his attorney, Rosemary Carroll, that he wanted to change his will.

After he was back a couple of months, on March 18th, Courtney dialed 911 and told the Seattle police that Kurt had locked himself in a room with a gun and was threatening suicide. This did not make the press when it happened. It only made the press after Cobain's body was discovered weeks later, dead in the greenhouse above his garage.

When I looked into the facts of the March incident, they turned out to be completely false. I got the police report and also spoke on the record from the detective that arrived on the scene that day, Everett Edwards. He was a patrol officer then but is now a detective. He told me that when he arrived at the scene that day, he found Courtney Love standing in a nightgown screaming wildly on the porch. Love told him that Cobain was upstairs in the house with a gun. But they found Cobain standing in the backyard with his hands in his pockets. He had no gun. He just looked deeply embarrassed and deeply annoyed. When they approached him, he just apologized, said that he didn't have a gun and that he didn't attempt suicide. He just got into a fight with his wife and locked himself in his bedroom.

When the officers interviewed Courtney Love, she actually admitted that she made the entire story up and that she had never seen Kurt with a gun. She had never heard him say that he was going to hurt himself. So, there we actually have "on the record" from the Seattle police department, Courtney Love inventing an entire suicide attempt by Kurt Cobain, just before he actually died.

Q. So, you are saying that she was actually setting up his murder then?

A. She was actually setting up. She was framing the suicide narrative.

Now, after that March 18 episode, on or around that day, it is police protocol for domestic violence 911 calls to confiscate any guns or drugs they could find, which they did. Cobain didn't have much of a security system at home. He didn't have any bodyguards, and he used to have a lot of strange groupies showing up at the house looking for him. So he had some real security concerns. So after that, he asked his best friend, Dylan Carlson, to purchase a shotgun for him in his name because he was afraid there would be another 911 call and the police would confiscate the shotgun. That was simply a home protection shotgun.

Shortly after that, Kurt Cobain decided to attend drug rehab in Los Angeles. He flew out with his best friend, Dylan Carlson, to a Los Angeles drug rehab center, and he stayed just a few days before they flew back on April 1st.

On April 4th, just one day after Courtney hired Tom Grant, she filed a missing persons police report from Los Angeles, but it was a false report. She filed it in her mother-in-law's name, Wendy O'Connor, with who Kurt had very little contact as they had a poor relationship. *"Mr. Cobain ran away from a California facility and flew back to Seattle. He also bought a shotgun and may be suicidal. Mr. Cobain may be at 'redacted address' for narcotics."* The story Courtney framed was that he fled from a California drug rehab facility, then bought the shotgun, and was intending suicide. But that's not true. The facility where he was staying in Los Angeles, he was free to come and go as he wanted. It was not a lockdown facility. He didn't have to run away from it. The shotgun he had purchased before he flew to Los Angeles, not when he returned.

The police never questioned it, and why should they because his own mother said it. But his mother never did say so. I think that was the consequential pebble that started the whole avalanche that Kurt Cobain committed suicide.

Q. Was there a suicide note or not?

A. There was a suicide note found at the scene, and it was written in red ink on the back of an IHOP menu.

The note was made public by Tom Grant and not Courtney Love. Excerpts of the note had appeared in the press – the very suicidal excerpts of the note. Tom actually tricked Courtney into giving him the note so that he could make a photocopy of it. What he discovered was that the note never mentioned suicide, and it actually reads as a retirement letter to Nirvana fans about the breakup of Nirvana. It never mentioned suicide. He doesn't even mention Courtney or his daughter, except for in the third person. And he signed the note with his full name, "Kurt Cobain." I don't think too many people sign their suicide note with their full names.

There's also a suspicious postscript. It's written in a different hand with a different pen. The postscript mentions Courtney. The postscript is the only place Courtney and the daughter are mentioned. So, it's a very suspicious suicide note, and it doesn't make any sense.

Now, Courtney gave the Rome suicide note to the Seattle police for a comparison writing sample. However, I think it was on June the 17th of 1994, the detective in charge of the investigation, Donald Cameron, personally drove to Courtney Love's home and returned the Rome note to her. He told her, "I would get rid of this note if I were you or destroy it immediately because it's not going to do you any good." That is according to Courtney Love herself.

Another thing is that when people are telling the truth, their alibi doesn't change over time. Their story always stays the same. Tom Grant's story, for instance, has never changed. People who are deceptive change their stories. They add things over time to enhance their believability.

So, we have two suicide notes, according to Courtney: the Rome note and the note found at the death scene. Then, later on in November or December, in an issue of

Rolling Stone magazine, she claimed there was a third suicide note.

About five years ago, she gave an interview with a guy named Mark Young, and she claimed that Kurt had made a fourth suicide note in December of 1993. She had never mentioned that before. So, that would make a total of four suicide notes from Kurt Cobain, according to Courtney Love. Only one of which has ever been made public. The notes continue to be a problem for her and continue to be a problem for the Seattle police.

Q. What was the issue with a credit card?

A. When Tom was first hired, he was hired on Easter Sunday. Courtney found his ad in the Yellow Pages in Los Angeles when she was staying in the Beverly Hills Peninsula Hotel, and she called him asking him to help her find out who was using her husband's stolen credit card.

When he arrived at her hotel suite that day, she told him that she had canceled the credit card and that she lied about his card being stolen. She simply just canceled all of his cards, credit, and ATM. She had competed for control over the finances. Why she did that was because she did not know where Kurt Cobain was, and she did not want him to leave Seattle. Because if he left Seattle alive, he would probably follow through on his plans to divorce her, and that would have been devastating to her career.

Tom then got the credit card information from the Seafirst Bank, and he started tracking the credit card activity. We believe that Kurt Cobain was probably killed on the late Sunday evening, April 3rd, or early morning of Monday, April 4th. But there were attempted transactions on the credit card all week long, mostly to withdraw money. There were two attempted withdrawals of money on Friday, April 8th, the day that the body was discovered. The card was never found, and after the body was discovered, it was never used again.

Q. Now you also claim that he was never barricaded in the room where he was found?

A. No, not at all. We spoke to, on the record, when the body was discovered, the fire department. They were called, and they forced entry into the garage where the body was. The fireman, John Fisk, who is now a lieutenant, broke a pane of glass and entered the door, which was a simple twist and lock door. He told us there was nothing in front of that door. There was no stool or anything, and it was very easy to enter the room.

Now there are two sets of police reports. In one of the reports, they mention that there was a small gardening stool in the greenhouse. There's sort of an amendment to the police report that says there was a gardening stool pushed up against the greenhouse door that was preventing access. Kurt Cobain had wedged the stool up against the door, and therefore he must have been alone inside the greenhouse when he died. But the fireman told us that was not true, and there was no stool there.

So, that was a blatant lie that we caught the Seattle police in.

John Fisk took the emergency call during a normal shift as a first responder paramedic and went for a run to the Cobain property. He was the first person to enter the greenhouse by breaking a glass panel on the locked French door. It was immediately evident to him that the person found was a case of DOA because there was a recognizable gunshot wound to the head with a pool of blood on the floor by Cobain's head.

Fisk recalls his involvement in the *Soaked in Bleach* interview on April 6, 2016, with the Mercer Island Reporter, who wrote, *"He reiterated to the producers that he still believes the case remains a suicide,"* and that Fisk calls himself a bit of a skeptic when it comes to conspiracy theories. He says conspiracies seem to come up with any celebrity death. He added, *"in a case of an obvious suicide, which from my limited experience with a crime scene, it looked like every other suicide I've seen."* But none of this was mentioned in the film.[5]

Q. What was there about the driver's license?

A. The first officer on the scene, Lemondowski, whose a lieutenant now, said Cobain's wallet was on the floor, and they pulled out his driver's license from the wallet. They put it on top of the wallet and took a photograph of it for identification purposes. A story got out in the press that Kurt Cobain had pulled his license out himself in order to help out the investigators when they found him.

Courtney Love had always promoted a gruesome depiction of Kurt's death by claiming there was lots of blood everywhere at the scene. But none of that was true. There was very little blood at the scene, actually. His face was very recognizable. There was very little damage to his face as it was a minimum impact shotgun. There was a rumor going around that the face was so badly damaged that the body had to be identified by fingerprints. But that's not true. The medical examiners fingerprint everybody no matter the condition of the body.

Q I've heard that Courtney was not acting like what a suicide survivor would normally do. Is that true?

A. Yes. Suicide survivors have a very difficult time. But it wasn't for her. The day that the body was discovered, she was actually on the phone for hours, calling reporters and arranging for reporters to come to the house. The next day she called MTV and gave an interview at length. Every day afterward, she was constantly on the phone with the press. She even gave Tom Grant's cell phone number out to the press so that they could get a quote from him. I was told that Courtney spent eight to 10 hours on the phone every day.

Q. You think the Seattle police are liable?

A. We think the possibility of the Seattle police being liable or sued is why they didn't want the case reopened. They wanted to wait until the statute of limitations for that has passed now.

Mike Ciesynski retired from the Seattle police department in 2017 after serving 37 years. Mike was assigned to the homicide unit for 22 years, 12 of which were in the cold case division. He was asked to review the case and after said the following:

"One of the original case detectives, Steve Kirkland, had passed away, as did the scene sergeant Don Cameron. Steve and his partner Jim Yoshida were the best homicide detectives in the unit. Jim was retired, so I gave him a call and told him what I was up to. Jim told me that Courtney Love was very cooperative throughout the investigation and that they had spent a lot of time on the case.

Dr. Nikolas Hartshome was the Assistant Medical Examiner who conducted the autopsy. Nick was a great guy who passed away in 2002. When I received the autopsy report, I remembered leaning back in my chair and giving a "whoa" after seeing the morphine level Kurt had in his system. It also showed track marks, and there were several grams of black tar heroin left in his kit. Black tar heroin is found on the west coast west of the Mississippi as compared to brown or white heroin found on the eastern part of the U.S.

The note recovered from the scene was examined by a Washington State Patrol Forensic Document Examiner, who concluded the note was written by Cobain. Detectives Kirkland and Yoshida had met with Kurt's mother, Wendy O'Connor, and showed her the note. She said she believed the note was written by Cobain.

I also decided to have a look at the shotgun. Some conspiracy theorists had suggested that Seattle Police Department had turned the shotgun over to Courtney Love or had destroyed it. When the rusted weapon was brought to me, and after I inspected it, I had a warehouseman photograph me holding the weapon.

Did I find any earth-shattering evidence that would change the Medical Examiner's conclusion that Kurt committed suicide? No. In fact, I found evidence that strengthened that finding.

I located the receipt for the purchased shotgun shells from a Seattle Gun store that matched the time and location where a Seattle cab driver said he dropped off a male matching Cobain's description after picking him up from the Cobain residence. Also, when I had questions about the positioning of the shotgun found in Cobain's hand and the location of the spent shell casing, I interviewed an experienced weapons armorer who explained the dynamics of what had likely occurred.[6]

Listen to the full interview with Matthew Richer on my website:

www.alanrwarren.com/hom-podcast-episodes/episode/b4042272/kurt-cobain-death-matthew-richer

---

1. Suicide of Kurt Cobain - Wikipedia. https://en.wikipedia.org/wiki/Kurt_Cobain_Was_Murdered
2. Kathleen O'Toole - Wikipedia. https://en.wikipedia.org/wiki/Kathleen_O%27Toole
3. Levi Pulkkinen, *Don Cameron, dead at 71: He investigated notorious deaths,* March 21, 2011 https://www.seattlepi.com/local/article/Don-Cameron-dead-at-71-He-investigated-1235743.php
4. Mike Cieysinski: *Kurt Cobain death: Detective who reviewed Kurt Cobain's death file details evidence,* April 5, 2019. https://www.cbsnews.com/news/kurt-cobain-death-detective-who-reviewed-kurt-cobains-case-file-details-evidence/
5. Silvia K.: *25th Anniversary of a Tragic Suicide & a Multimorbid Conspiracy Theory (Update),* April 5, 2019. knowsnotwhatitmeans.blogspot.com/2019/04/multimorbid.html
6. https://wdef.com/2019/04/05/detective-reviewed-kurt-cobains-death-file-details-evidence/

Suicide Note
INTERVIEW WITH DR. CAROL CHASKI

Carole Elisabeth Chaski is a forensic linguist considered one of the leading experts in her field. Her research has led to improvements in the methodology and reliability of stylometric analysis and inspired further research on using this approach for authorship identification. In the undergraduate textbook, *Forensic Linguistics: Second Edition: An Introduction To Language, Crime and the Law*, John Olsson wrote, "The first linguist to consider markedness in terms of authorship systematically was Carole Chaski, whose statistical analysis of syntax in authorship has met the Daubert challenge in the U.S. court system." Chaski's methodology, according to Olsson, includes software that uses four grammar rules to identify a text's syntactic markedness, in combination with measurements of the ways punctuation is used by a writer.

Olsson continued, *"Chaski should be credited with having brought forensic authorship comparison as opposed to long text authorship "attribution" into the scientific arena, and out of the darkness of literary criticism, canonical literary corpus construction and discourse analysis modes of authorship identification."* Her contributions have served as expert testimony in several federal and state court cases in the United States and Canada. She is president of ALIAS Technology and executive director of the Institute for Linguistic Evidence, a non-profit research organization devoted to linguistic evidence.

Chaski is known for her research on the reliability of different variables, such as spelling and syntax, in forensic linguists' analysis of discriminants amongst unknown authors. She concluded that many of the frequently measured variables, such as the number of spelling errors or prescriptive grammar errors in a sample, were not accurate ways of determining authorship or discriminating between suspected authors.

Chaski's criticism was based on how the variation within many of these variables reflects dialects and not idiolects. Tim Grant and Kevin Baker have criticized Chaski's evaluation of the authorship markers, addressing issues with the reliability and validity of her methods for evaluating each marker. They also draw attention to Chaski's selection of authors, namely because they lack sociolinguistic diversity. [1] The interview was in 2016.

Q. How did you find yourself involved in suicide notes?

A. I got a call from a detective named W. Allison Blackman. He goes by Allison, his family name, asking me if there was any way that I could determine the authorship of suicide notes that were left on a home computer of three guys that lived together as roommates. So, I asked him if he had any ink, any paper, or any writing, thinking that he would have gone to the state lab. He said that he had already done that, and they told me if you don't have ink, you don't have paper or handwriting, what would you expect them to do.

He started to ask around and found out there was a thing called linguistics. That's when he called up my department, and somebody sent him to me. I told him that if he was going to work with me as an experiment, I had some ideas. But he would have to recognize that this was all experimental, and he was okay with that.

I analyzed the syntactic patterns of the three roommates. By syntax, I mean by the way we put our words and phrases into sentences. If you can remember diagramming in middle school, it's kind of like that. Then I counted up things about those syntactic patterns and ran a very simple statistical test. And there was only one in ten thousand chance that the fellow had written his own suicide note. There was a significant difference between the suicide notes and one of his roommates and not the other roommate. So, I said I think this is the fellow who wrote the suicide notes because I can't get any significant difference between him and the suicide notes.

That's when they told me that he had access to all the legal drugs that were injected into the fellow that died. He was six weeks from his medical degree. He was known to be able to give medicine without waking people up. He was arrested and went on trial. On the witness stand, he admitted that he wrote the suicide notes.

Q. So it's not forensic psychology. It's forensic linguistics?

A. Absolutely, you hit it on the head.

Q. You don't analyze the handwriting. You analyze the thought behind it and say that this mindset belongs to this person?

A. Yes. I don't analyze the handwriting. Or I don't analyze the psychology of the person behind it either. I don't say that the person is depressed because I'm not a psychologist. I can't really make that kind of announcement. What I can say is that the language, which is built in their minds first, takes our thoughts and encodes them somehow. So, I can say that those patterns either match or don't match some other documents.

One of the things about language that I really love is how forgiving it is. For instance, you know how we can start a sentence, and if we really know somebody well, that person can finish it for us. When you are reading some things, it's as if you can hear them. But if you don't hear them, you can think there's something fishy here.

That's how language is. It's built so that we can communicate super-fast with each other and also kind of predict what's coming next. Syntax is really the glue that holds that together, but syntax also degrades in milliseconds. Everyone has had the experience like it's almost a joke in marriage counseling, "Bob, say exactly what Mary just said." Then he paraphrases it. We all paraphrase when we hear what somebody just said. The syntax is lost, and you just remember the meaning of it, and then you say the meaning in however you would say it.

Q. How does the court deal with this? Are there any admissibility issues with it?

A. Yes. I'm so glad you brought this up. Fortunately, the method I developed using these syntactic patterns has been very successful in being admitted to a court in the states and also in federal court. But that's because we've been developing these methods for years. We started back in 1994 with developing. We were really conscious of figuring it out when it was wrong and what does it need to work well. So, these days in an American court, judges typically go by what is the Daubert Standard. Some of the things that the Daubert standard wants are your error rate or how often your method is wrong. Also, are you following a standard operating procedure?

In United States federal law, the "Daubert standard" is a rule of evidence regarding the admissibility of expert witness testimony. A party may raise a Daubert motion, a special motion *in limine* raised before or during the trial, to exclude the presentation of unqualified evidence to the jury. The Daubert trilogy is the three United States Supreme Court cases that articulated the Daubert standard:

Daubert v. Merrell Dow Pharmaceuticals, Inc. in 1993, which held that Rule 702 of the Federal Rules of Evidence did not incorporate the Frye standard as a basis for assessing the admissibility of scientific expert testimony but that the rule incorporated a flexible reliability standard instead.

General Electric Co. v. Joiner in 1997, which held that a district court judge may exclude expert testimony when there are gaps between the evidence relied on by an expert and that person's conclusion and that an abuse-of-discretion standard of review is the proper standard for appellate courts to use in reviewing a trial court's decision of whether it should admit expert testimony.

Kumho Tire Co. v. Carmichael in 1999, which held

that the judge's gatekeeping function identified in Daubert applies to all expert testimony, including that which is non-scientific.[2]

So, we have that for the syntactic author technique. There are also other methods out there. There's stylistic, which is sometimes called sociolinguistics. It has had a rough time being admitted because it doesn't have an error rating or standard operating method. Sometimes you are allowed to tell the jury, but you can't offer a conclusion about it.

We have about a 95 percent accuracy rate with the syntactic method. We, first of all, run it on the different suspects in the case and decide how accurately we can differentiate each person. If I can't differentiate the known suspects, what good is it to do with the unknown suspects?

The stylistic method hasn't done that. The reality is that they can't do it. The stylistic method is so subjective that they state, "We don't know what we're going to find until we find it." I would say these two methods are comparing scientific evidence and non-scientific subjective evidence.

The stylistic method is too general. For instance, in a suicide note, the person could have used the "+" sign or "&" sign instead of "and," therefore, anybody that uses one of those symbols could be a suspect. One person using the stylistic method could say, "The person using one of these symbols is very important. The next person using it could say it has no significance at all." That's what's scary about that method and why the courts are not letting it in.

Q. How often do people leave suicide notes? Do we know that?

A. That's pretty rare, actually. The numbers range from 10 to 25 percent.

Q. I didn't realize that it was so low. You would have thought that the person killing themselves would have wanted their survivors to know why they killed themselves.

A. I know. I think that for the survivors, this is the most difficult thing. From 75 to 90 percent of them, they didn't get that kind of closure. Suicide notes are rare. Suicide notes are so variable they're almost like human faces. They are so unique in that they just don't share a lot of features over and over. When people who are not suicidal try to think about what they would say in a suicide note, that's very different from what real suicidal people write in their suicide notes.

Q. Then is it safe to say that suicide isn't really well thought out?

A. I think there can be impulsive suicides. In the literature that I have read, most of the time, it's very shocking to the people around the person who committed suicide. It's not too often that people say, "Oh yeah, I saw that coming." The closest to that is some people might say, "I thought he was getting better," or "I thought he was getting happier."

This is because there's this terrible period of tension when the person is deciding what it is they are going to do. Once they make the decision, they actually do get happier because they know now. They've got that resolution, that calmness. So, everyone around them mistakenly thinks that the resolution and calmness mean they are okay. When really the decision has been made the other way.

Q. Fake suicide notes. In most movies and television, you always see the culprit killing somebody and leaving a faked suicide note behind to try and fool the police. Is this something that you see in real life a lot?

A. That was my first case, actually. The faked suicide note that I mentioned earlier, the man who killed his roommate and wrote the fake suicide note, he admitted on the witness stand that he wrote the note to get the cops off his back. I have had cases where the police theorized that the suicide note was fake because they thought a guy murdered his girlfriend. But when I analyzed the note, it was a real suicide note. I think police officers have to think about it both ways. Could this be a real suicide note or a fake one?

Q. I'm sure that when the person who killed themselves is famous, there's always going to be controversial questions asked. So, when we talk about Kurt Cobain's death, there are a lot of people who really hate Courtney Love, his wife at the time, and therefore there are lots of rumors that she was somehow involved and that he could never have killed himself. You appeared in Tom Grant's documentary *Soaked in Bleach?*

A. Yes.

Q. You have made some comments since that appearance saying that they manipulated what you had actually said in the show. Can you explain what you mean by that?

A. Yes.

Q. What exactly is it that they changed?

A. Basically, I am presented as saying that it was not a real suicide note. And that the suicide note was just stereotypical language, and anyone could have written it. What I believe and what they presented are two different things. Actually, I ran the note three ways through my software I developed for identifying suicide notes, SNARE (Suicide Note Assessment Research).

SNARE works by looking for the linguistic patterns that are associated with suicide notes and also with a bunch of control documents. Sometimes suicide notes sound like love letters. Sometimes it sounds like an apology or business letters even. They can also be trauma narratives. That's one of the reasons they can be so hard to identify because they are all over the place. They are not stereotypical the way we normally think they should be. So, we go through the text analysis, which is done by computer, and it finds these patterns and counts them up.

Then we apply a statistical procedure to it, which decides if the note is on the side of real suicide notes or is it on the side of a control document like love letters, trauma narratives, those kinds of things. That software is about 86 percent accurate when the note is short, like 45 words or less. It's about 81 percent accurate when the note is very long, which makes sense when you think about it because the longer the note, it can become like one of the control documents. It can become like a trauma document, a really long apology. The short notes just don't have that room.

Q. What did the result of the Cobain note?

A. I ran the Cobain note, the whole note, the whole page, and it came out as a real suicide note. Then I ran the top three-quarters of it, which everyone seems to notice about the note because there's a division between the top three quarters and the bottom quarter. So, the top three quarter came out as a suicide note, and then the bottom quarter came out as a suicide note as well.

Q. Are you saying that he wrote it at two different times?

A. You know I thought about this, and I said this when I was being filmed for *Soaked in Bleach,* but it was cut. He wrote a very poetic first suicide note where in the first part of it, he talked about his career, his love of music, and his real disgust and hatred of the music industry. Also, the feeling that he wasn't being fair to his fans because he really hated what his life was like and his inability to cope with it very well. Then he wrote a more stereotypical suicide note at the bottom. But when you think about it, he killed himself twice too. He overdosed himself, and then he shot himself. So, his suicide is very much like a metaphor.

Q. Do you think it is possible that when he was considering his suicide, he wrote that first part of the note, then thought secondly about it and put the note away? He thought that he wasn't ready to do it, then later, when he was ready to do it, he wrote the second portion when he actually did it?

A. I haven't heard anything ever against that theory. In fact, you're the first person I ever heard propose that theory. I wouldn't know. I think the only way anybody could have tested that would have been ink analysis of the two different sections, and I don't even know who has the original document anymore. But that could have been one way to do it.

Q. The documentary tried to present that Courtney Love wrote that note and copied his writing.

A. Yes.

Q. There was also another person who appeared in the film, a forensics document expert Heidi Harralson, who also says that the film changed her interview as well, making it look like she said the note was traced to Courtney Love, and that's not what she really said.

Another expert interviewed for the film was Heidi Harralson, a Forensic Document Examiner. Her interview is played out while an animation of letters from the practice sheet appears to be placed perfectly over the letters at the bottom of the suicide note. Harralson watched a small part of *Soaked in Bleach* and stated, "Because I haven't seen the entire film, I can't critically evaluate it other than to say that I think what I said was mischaracterized through editing and taken out of context."[3]

A. Yes, I was really surprised that so many of us had the same experience with the *Soaked in Bleach* film. I knew that about Heidi. I know her. I knew that about another person in the film. When I look back at it now, it's pretty obvious that there was a struggle going on among the directors or producers where they would ask questions in one way but then talk in another way off camera. I was just told to say what I had done, and that's what I did. I talked about SNARE and how it's been validated on more than 400 suicide notes, and so we know the error rate. SNARE's got a really good error rate from 14 to 20 percent.

Q. When we take the case of Kurt Cobain, who was very well-liked, and his wife Courtney Love, who was not, the public assumes she had something to do with it even though there's no hard evidence of it. How often do you come across this?

A. I think that in many of these cases, the conclusion is politically motivated. Now I'm using that term politically in a really broad sense. What I mean is there are all kinds of other reasons that make the decision that it is a suicide, or it is not suicide, the favored one.

I had a case with a very high-ranking military officer, and he had been involved in some pretty high-profile missions in the Middle

East. It was concluded by a military investigation that he committed suicide. Part of the argument was because of the last email he sent to his wife. His wife contacted me, and I ran the note through SNARE. It was not a suicide note, and I wrote my analysis up, but the military was not interested in hearing from me. It was because the thought of this guy being murdered was just too hot of a political issue given where he was stationed at the time and what it said about our base security and what it said about infiltration. It was just easier for the military to say it was suicide, and of course, a marine would shoot himself with the wrong hand in the head. I found that out after I did the analysis and his wife said to me he would never use his wrong hand for shooting. No gun residue testing was done on him. It was really a very incomplete crime scene investigation. But it goes back to what you were saying, if there's a very popular attitude of what it should have been, then it's very easy to not be thorough.

Q. Well, there's a lot of people who loved Kurt Cobain, and I don't think they really wanted to hear the truth that he actually killed himself. It's easier to blame someone who you hate.

A. Yes.

Q. It really looks like that film *Soaked in Bleach* was trying to present the case that Courtney Love murdered Cobain and actually edited their guests' evidence to look like they all agreed with that theory. Not only is it wrong to create false evidence in a murder case, but it also hurts the guests that were on the show because then you are forever out there trying to get it corrected in public.

A. Yes. For me, it is such an honor to be on your show to speak freely about it because I do feel my words were twisted. Thank you very much for giving me the opportunity.

Q. When I contacted Tom Grant, he told me he would only do the show if we paid him. Isn't the truth more important than money? In his case, obviously not. He is behind the film. It's really important to put out the real evidence. The next thing he wanted was for us to put him on with Courtney Love as well.

A. Yes. It's really crucial to have unbiased information. That's one of the good things about having the SNARE software. It has no skin in the game, no feelings about the people involved or the music.

SUICIDE NOTE

Boddah

...ing from the tongue of an experienced simpleton who obviously would rather be an emasculated, infantile complainee. This note should be pretty easy to understand. All the warnings from the punk rock 101 courses over the years, since my first introduction to the, shall we say, ethics of independence and the embracement of your community has proven to be very true. I haven't felt the excitement of listening to as well as creating music along with reading and writing for too many years now. I feel guilty beyond words about these things. For example when we're backstage and the lights go out and the manic roar of the crowds begins, it doesn't affect me the way in which it did for Freddie Mercury, who seemed to relish in the love and adoration from the crowd, which is something I totally admire and envy. The fact is, I can't fool you. Any one of you. It simply isn't fair to you or me. The worst crime I can think of would be to rip people off by faking it and pretending as if I'm having 100% fun. Sometimes I feel as if I should have a punch-in time clock before I walk out on stage. I've tried everything within my power to appreciate it (and I do, God, believe me I do, but it's not enough). I appreciate the fact that I and we have affected and entertained a lot of people. I must be one of those narcissists who only appreciate things when they're gone or about to be gone. I'm too sensitive. I need to be slightly numb in order to regain the enthusiasm I once had as a child. On our last 3 tours, I've had a much better appreciation for all the people I've known personally, and as fans of our music, but I still can't get over the frustration, the guilt and empathy I have for everyone. There's good in all of us and I think I simply love people too much, so much that it makes me feel too fucking sad. The sad little, sensitive, unappreciative, Pisces, Jesus man! Why don't you just enjoy it? I don't know! I have a goddess of a wife who sweats ambition and empathy and a daughter who reminds me too much of what I used to be, full of love and joy, kissing every person she meets because everyone is good and will do her no harm. And that terrifies me to the point to where I can barely function. I can't stand the thought of Frances becoming the miserable self-destructive, death rocker that I've become. I have it good, very good, and I'm grateful, but since the age of seven, I've become hateful towards all humans in general. Only because it seems so easy for people to get along and have empathy. Empathy! Only because I love and feel sorry for people too much I guess. Thank you all from the pit of my burning, nauseous stomach for your letters and concern during the past years. I'm too much of an erratic, moody baby! I don't have the passion anymore, and so remember, it's better to burn out than to fade away.

peace, love, Empathy. Kurt Cobain

Frances and Courtney, I'll be at your altar.
Please keep going Courtney, for Frances
for her life which will be so much happier
without me. I LOVE YOU, I LOVE YOU

Listen to the full interview with Dr. Carol Chaski on my website:

www.alanrwarren.com/hom-podcast-episodes/episode/c38343c0/kurt-cobains-death-dr-carol-chaski

1. Carole Chaski - Wikipedia. https://en.wikipedia.org/wiki/Carole_Chaski
2. https://en.wikipedia.org/wiki/Daubert_standard
3. Frank E.: *The Aftermath of "Soaked in Bleach" - Part II,* June 27, 2016. https://knowsnotwhatitmeans.blogspot.com/2016/06/the-aftermath-of-soaked-in-bleach-part.html

PART II
Marilyn Monroe

Marilyn Monroe was born Norma Jeane Mortenson on June 1, 1926, and died on August 4, 1962. She was an American actress, model, and singer. She became one of the most popular sex symbols of the 1950s and early 1960s and was emblematic of the era's changing attitudes towards sexuality.

She was a top-billed actress for only a decade, but her films grossed $200 million, which is the equivalent to $2 billion in 2019. Long after her death, she continues to be a major icon of pop culture. In 1999, the American Film Institute ranked Monroe sixth on its list of the greatest female screen legends from Hollywood's "Golden Age."[1]

Marriages

On January 14, 1954, she and Joe DiMaggio were married at the San Francisco City Hall. They then traveled to Japan, combining a honeymoon with his business trip. From Tokyo, she traveled alone to Korea, where she participated in a USO show, singing songs from her films for over 60,000 U.S. Marines over four days. After returning to the U.S., Monroe settled with Fox in March, with the promise of a new contract, a bonus of $100,000, and a starring role in the film adaptation of the Broadway success, *The Seven Year Itch*. In September 1954, Monroe began filming and starred opposite Tom Ewell, as a woman who becomes the object of her married neighbor's sexual fantasies. Although the film was shot in Hollywood, the studio decided to generate advance publicity by staging the filming of a scene on Lexington Avenue in Manhattan in which Monroe stood on a subway grate with the air blowing up the skirt of her white dress. The shoot lasted several hours and attracted nearly 2,000 spectators. The "subway grate scene" became one of Monroe's most famous, and *The Seven Year Itch* became one of the biggest commercial successes of the year after its release in June 1955. The publicity stunt placed Monroe on international front pages, and it also marked the end of her marriage to DiMaggio, who was infuriated by it. The marriage had been troubled from the start by his jealousy and controlling attitude, and he was also physically abusive. After returning from NYC to Hollywood in October 1954, Monroe filed for divorce after only nine months of marriage.

In June 1956, playwright Arthur Miller left his first wife, Mary Slattery, whom he had married in 1940, and wed film star, Marilyn Monroe. They had met in 1951, had a brief affair, and remained in contact since then. Monroe had just turned 30 when they married. She never had a real family of her own and was eager to join the family of her new husband. Monroe converted to Judaism, which led Egypt to ban all of her films.

In August, Monroe began filming *The Prince and the Showgirl* at Pinewood Studios in England. It was to be directed, co-produced, and co-starred by Laurence Olivier. The production was complicated by conflicts between Olivier and Monroe. Olivier, who had also directed and starred in the stage play, angered her with the patronizing statement "All you have to do is be sexy." With his demand, she replicated Vivien Leigh's stage interpretation of the character. Monroe experienced other problems during the production. Her dependence on pharmaceuticals escalated, and, according to author Donald Spoto, who penned her biography, she had a miscarriage. After returning from England, Monroe took an

18-month hiatus to concentrate on family life. She and Miller split their time between NYC, Connecticut, and Long Island. She had an ectopic pregnancy in mid-1957 and a miscarriage a year later. These problems were most likely linked to her endometriosis. Monroe was also briefly hospitalized due to a barbiturate overdose.

Monroe's last film was John Huston's *The Misfits*, which Miller had written to provide her with a dramatic role. Miller began writing the screenplay for *The Misfits* in 1960. It was directed by John Huston and starred Monroe. But it was during the filming that Miller and Monroe's relationship hit difficulties, and he later said that the filming was one of the lowest points in his life. Shortly before the film's premiere in 1961, Miller and Monroe divorced after their five years of marriage.[2]

Nineteen months later, August 5, 1962, Monroe died of a likely drug overdose.

Death

Monroe lived at 12305 Fifth Helena Drive in the Brentwood neighborhood of Los Angeles during her final months. Her housekeeper, Eunice

Murray, was staying overnight on the evening of August 4, 1962. Murray awoke at 3:00 a.m. on August 5th and sensed something was wrong. She saw light from under Monroe's bedroom door but could not get a response and found the door locked.

Murray then called Monroe's psychiatrist, Dr. Ralph Greenson, who arrived at the house shortly after and broke into the bedroom through a window to find Monroe dead in her bed. Monroe's physician, Dr. Hyman Engelberg, arrived at around 3:50 a.m. and pronounced her dead at the scene. At 4:25 a.m., the LAPD was notified.

Monroe died between 8:30 p.m. and 10:30 p.m. on August 4th, and the toxicology report showed that the cause of death was acute barbiturate poisoning. She had 8 mg chloral hydrate and 4.5 mg of pentobarbital Nembutal in her blood, and 13 mg of pentobarbital in her liver. Empty medicine bottles were found next to her bed. The possibility that Monroe had accidentally overdosed was ruled out because the dosages found in her body were several times over the lethal limit.

The Los Angeles County Coroner's Office was assisted in their investigation by the Los Angeles Suicide Prevention Team, who had expert knowledge on suicide. Monroe's doctors stated that she had been "prone to severe fears and frequent depressions" with "abrupt and unpredictable mood changes" and had overdosed several times in the past, possibly intentionally. Due to these facts and the lack of any indication of foul play, Deputy Coroner, Thomas Noguchi, classified her death as a probable suicide.

In the following decades, several conspiracy theories, including murder and accidental overdose, have been introduced to contradict suicide as the cause of Monroe's death. The speculation that Monroe had been murdered first gained mainstream attention with the publication of Norman Mailer's *Marilyn: A Biography* in 1973, and in the following years became widespread enough for the Los Angeles County District Attorney John Van de Kamp to conduct a threshold investigation in 1982 to see whether a criminal investigation should be opened. No evidence of foul play was found.[3]

---

1. https://en.wikipedia.org/wiki/Marilyn_Monroe
2. Arthur Miller - Wikipedia. https://en.wikipedia.org/wiki/Timebends
3. *American actress Marilyn Monroe is found dead at her home from a drug overdose, August 5, 1962.* https://historicnewsclippings.com/8-5-1962marilyn-monroe-overdose/

Declassified
INTERVIEW WITH PAUL DAVID

American filmmaker and producer Paul Davids' films are known for controversy. Beginning with *Roswell,* a 1994 nominee for Golden Globe as Best TV Motion Picture, which he executive produced and co-wrote as a Showtime original movie. It dealt with issues of extraterrestrial life and the purported "truth embargo" on the subject of ET contact.

Davids' many books and films enjoyed a 2018 resurgence. His film, *The Sci-Fi Boys* starring Peter Jackson, was on display through September 2018 at the Pasadena History Museum in their exhibit called "Dreaming the Universe." *Jesus in India* had an

Italian premiere at the Odeon Theater in Florence, Italy, in May that year. His film *The Life After Death Project* was featured in June at the Fortfest in Baltimore, a Fortean conference. Paul also presented on the follow-up book to that film, *An Atheist in Heaven: The Ultimate Evidence for Life After Death*.

His film, *Marilyn Monroe Declassified*, "balances the image of the blonde bombshell icon we thought we knew with information about her revealed in newly declassified FBI and CIA files. Here is the proof that her troubles were not all the product of her upbringing in an orphanage, abuse of prescription drugs, and failed marriages. Beginning with her wedding to Communist-leaning playwright Arthur Miller, for whom she converted to Judaism, she was tailed, targeted, and tormented by the FBI, CIA, and Mafia. Ultimately, through affairs with powerful men, she was unwittingly caught in the middle of a vendetta of lethal forces. Dead at age 36, just months after singing "Happy Birthday, Mr. President" at JFK's extravagant party, she was officially listed as a "probable suicide." The film makes a powerful case for the idea that the official conclusion was wrong. The film featured an interview with Greg Schreiner and Pierre Vudrag, Paul Davids on *Bigger Questions*."[1]

Q. How did you get into Marilyn Monroe and her death enough to make a film about it?

A. Well, I had recently finished the *Life After Death Project* film, and it was on Sci-Fi. It was an examination of a particularly fascinating case about life after death. I was always aware that there was quite a controversy about Marilyn Monroe's death, which had been ruled at the time, in 1962, a probable suicide. Yet the controversy and objection to that started almost immediately. So, it has always been in the back of my mind, and I thought that maybe the circumstances of her death were unresolved and covered up.

Since I was curious about the realm of spirit communication from the afterlife and had had an experience with a psychic detective, Dorothy Allison, when I was the producer of F. Lee Bailey's *The Lie Detector*

Show, I had a very open mind to the possibility. Someone suggested that Marilyn's spirit was very disquieted because people still think she committed suicide, and she didn't.

So, that was one thing. The other thing was that I happened to be invited to film original color separation negatives. These are very, very large negatives that are in bullet-proof plastic. There were over 20 of them of Marilyn's Golden Dreams Calendar photos, which was the famous nude that was controversial from very early on in her career. When I filmed those, there were other people present that talked about the history of Marilyn's life. I thought that maybe there's something real here. This could become an original feature documentary.

Q. How did you deal with all of the rumors and conspiracies about Marilyn? Was it easy to separate the real from the fake?

A. There was a fake news story within the last year declaring a CIA agent who had confessed on his death bed to having murdered Marilyn. It had clues that it was made up because it talked about her affair with Fidel Castro, which is completely absurd. But people don't know right away that when these fake stories come out, they are being used. And that they need to be completely dismissed. That was pretty much an easy one because it came from a known site for those kinds of things. I'm very cautious about what to accept.

In *Marilyn Declassified*, I've got really firm evidence from the real people, the witnesses, their testimonies, and statements that go back to the year of her death. I'm dealing with the people who were actually involved and what they had to say, and how it changed over the years. There were secrets kept that people began to recant after about 20 years, and they changed what they said. Their changes had become more consistent with other things that we know that made us feel that there was a massive cover-up.

There were two police chiefs of Los Angeles, Daryl Gates and Tom Reddin, who both indicated a cover-up years after. Well, Daryl Gates now indicates that Bobby Kennedy had been in town on the day of her death. That's something Bobby Kennedy had always denied. So, you have to ask why. Why was his presence in Los Angeles being covered up at that time? Tom Reddin, the other police chief, said that Marilyn's death was handled as a top-secret intelligence operation, which meant that there was disinformation issued and that facts were withheld. So, you want to get to the source, the original people. Then, find out what's new and what do I add to this mystery that's been going on all these years.

Thomas Reddin was a Los Angeles Police Department chief from 1967 to 1969. He left on May 6, 1969, to become a news commentator. He also owned a private security company in Los Angeles called the Tom Reddin Security. Reddin helped modernize the department and introduced the community policing concept, which "perceives the community as an agent and partner in promoting security rather than as a passive audience." During his tenure, he allowed his department to give technical advice for the first three seasons of the revived version of the Jack Webb-created detective drama, *Dragnet*, and he even made an appearance at the end of the Season Two finale, "The Big Problem," in a plea for improved community relations between the department and the city and during the first season of the police drama, *Adam-12*.[2]

Daryl Gates was the Chief of the Los Angeles Police Department from 1978 to 1992. His length of tenure was second only to that of William H. Parker. As Chief of Police, he took a hardline, aggressive, paramilitary approach to law enforcement. Gates is co-credited with creating SWAT teams with LAPD's John Nelson, who others claim was the originator of SWAT in 1965. Gates also co-founded D.A.R.E. along with the Los Angeles Unified School District. After the Rodney King beating and the riots afterward, Gates retired from the police department. He was attributed with much of the blame.[3]

Then in recent years, there's been the release of FBI documents on Marilyn. Things that had been classified that we didn't have access to. Same as the CIA because both the FBI and the CIA watched her. She had attracted the interest of both of those agencies. So, I felt that someone had to put all of this together like a jigsaw puzzle. It's a great mystery, but can sense be made of it? And can we tell who the players are and who the actors are? Was Marilyn, in fact, murdered? I've concluded absolutely yes. No question that it was a contract killing. So, who was involved, and what can we learn about that? Years of research.

Q. On the previous show that we recorded, guest Jay Margolis claimed that RFK was behind the murder. I noticed that Milo Speriglio in *Crypt 33* seemed to have the same opinion. What is your opinion on that?

Milo A. Speriglio was a private detective hired to look into the death of Natalie Wood. But it was his involvement a few years later in the Marilyn Monroe death case that really put Speriglio on the map. Speriglio investigated Monroe's suicide for more than two decades and argued that she was the victim of a Chicago mob hit ordered by President John F. Kennedy's family members. He wrote three books on the subject. In *Crypt 33, The Saga Of Monroe*, Speriglio and another Los Angeles Private Investigator, Gregory Adela, recounted their evidence. At the age of 62, Milo died of lung cancer on April 30, 2000, at his home in Los Angeles.

> A. Well, actually, let's take them one at a time. Let's talk about Milo first and *Crypt 33*. He talked about Bobby Kennedy's involvement with Marilyn. In fact, he claims she became pregnant by Bobby Kennedy, and there was an abortion in the months before her death. He had promised to get a divorce from Ethel and marry Marilyn. She became upset and threatened to become public about a lot of things. He

never pointed the finger at Bobby Kennedy as being responsible for her death. But he certainly was a party interest.

Now, Margolis has a very good book. I disagree with parts of its conclusions. That's fine. You can pick and choose between us. I do not think that Bobby Kennedy was responsible for her death. I do believe that he was at her house that afternoon. We know from the housekeeper, from what she finally testified to, that there was quite an argument that day between them and that they both had become very upset.

But we know a lot more than that. And it makes us look in other directions for who did it. I know that Margolis placed a lot of emphasis on the testimony of the housekeeper's nephew. Her nephew, Norman Jeffries, I think his name was, had a lot of things to say years later. He claimed that Bobby Kennedy returned later that night with a couple of other people, and that was when Marilyn was murdered.

But if you want to go to *Crypt 33* again for a minute, he says no, and that it was a mob hit. He names the three hitmen as to who ordered it. Well, it was a mob hit, so it was ordered by Sam Giancana.

Samuel Mooney Giancana was an American mobster who was the boss of the Chicago Outfit from 1957 to 1966. According to some sources, Giancana and the Mafia were involved in John F. Kennedy's victory in the 1960 presidential election. During the 1960s, he was recruited by the Central Intelligence Agency in a plot to assassinate Cuban leader Fidel Castro. Conspiracy theorists consider Giancana, along with Mafia leaders Santo Trafficante Jr. and Carlos Marcello, associated with Kennedy's assassination. In 1965, Giancana was convicted of contempt of court, serving one year in prison. After his release from prison, Giancana fled to Cuernavaca, Mexico. In 1974, he was deported to the United States, returning to Chicago. Giancana was murdered on June 19, 1975, in Oak Park, Illinois, shortly before he was scheduled to appear before the Church Committee.[4]

I conclude this because there was a confession by close relatives of Sam Giancana who came forward in a book called *Double Cross* and said that Sam Giancana had confessed to them before he died. But he said that he was ordered at the behest of the CIA and that it was really a CIA contract to the mob.

Double Cross: The Explosive Inside Story of the Mobster Who Controlled America was written by mob boss Sam Giancana's brother Chuck Giancana, and nephew, also Sam. "According to the book, one of the most feared Chicago mobsters, Sam Giancana, clawed his way to the top of the Mafia hierarchy by starting as a hitman for Al Capone. He partied with major stars such as Frank Sinatra and Marilyn Monroe and did business with agents ranging from the CIA to the Vatican to the Shah of Iran. They also claim that the CIA asked Giancana to assassinate Fidel Castro. The book includes Giancana's testimony about the truth of his involvement in the deaths of Monroe and others. Chuck Giancana contributes a unique perspective of the mob's relationship with the Bay of Pigs and many other pivotal events of the 60s and beyond. *Double Cross* is an eye-opening account of the interworking of the government and the mob and how this relationship has impacted American history."5

> They did that in those days. We know that. That's history that you can research. Check out the mob's involvement on behalf of the CIA in an attempt to assassinate Fidel Castro. Trujillo was assassinated. Look into those details, and you will see that the CIA used the "at arm's length" as a hit squad when they didn't want something traced back to them.

Rafael Leónidas Trujillo Molina, nicknamed "El Jefe," or "The Chief," or "The Boss," was a Dominican dictator who ruled the Dominican Republic from February 1930 until his assassination in May 1961. On Tuesday, May 30, 1961, Trujillo was shot and killed when his blue 1957 Chevrolet Bel Air was ambushed on the road outside the Dominican capital. He was the victim of an ambush plotted by a number of men, such as General Juan Tomás Díaz, Pedro Livio Cedeño, Antonio de la Maza, Amado García Guerrero, and General Antonio Imbert Barrera. However, the plotters failed to take control as the later-executed General José René Román Fernandez betrayed his co-conspirators by his inactivity, and contingency plans had not been made. The role of the CIA in the killing has been debated. General Imbert Barrera insists that the plotters acted on their own. However, Trujillo was certainly murdered with weapons supplied by the CIA. In a 1975 report to the Deputy Attorney General of the United States, CIA officials described the agency as having no active part in the assassination and only a faint connection with the groups that planned the killing. However, the report is contradicted by later evidence.[6]

Now, was Giancana telling the truth? A CIA document surfaced signed by the head of counterintelligence, James Angleton, back in 1962. It matches very, very closely with the Sam Giancana confession.

James Jesus Angleton was chief of CIA Counterintelligence from 1954 to 1975. His official position within the organization was Associate Deputy Director of Operations for Counterintelligence. Angleton was significantly involved in the US response to the purported KGB defectors Anatoliy Golitsyn and Yuri Nosenko.[7]

As far as concern, Marilyn was going to go public about some things that were top secret that she wasn't supposed to know. That concern was there. These pieces link up in a way that I think Margolis hasn't put together. Now, who's right?

Q. But wouldn't JFK know that he was sharing secrets with Marilyn that would threaten her life?

A. He was probably aware but careless. He had a lot of mistresses and a number of them he talked to. Mary Pinchot Meyer, a mistress for a long time, was assassinated a year after his death right when the Warren Commission Report was coming out. She knew too much.

Mary Eno Pinchot Meyer was an American painter who lived in Washington D.C. She was married to Central Intelligence Agency official Cord Meyer from 1945–1958 and became involved romantically with President John F. Kennedy after her divorce from Meyer. Pinchot Meyer was shot to death on the Chesapeake & Ohio Canal towpath on October 12, 1964. A suspect, Ray Crump, Jr., was arrested and charged with her murder but was ultimately acquitted. Pinchot Meyer's life, her relationship with Kennedy, and her murder have been the subjects of numerous articles and books.[8]

There was Judith Exner Campbell. She was a go-between JFK and Sam Giancana because they had business together. The mob had helped put Kennedy in the White House by delivering Chicago. Yet the Kennedy administration, through Bobby

Kennedy, moved fiercely against the mobsters and tried to put them behind bars.

Judith Exner was an American woman who claimed to be the mistress of U.S. president John F. Kennedy and Mafia leaders Sam Giancana and John Roselli. She was also known as Judith Campbell Exner and Judith Campbell. In 1977, Exner published *Judith Exner: My Story*. In her memoir, she said that her relationship with Kennedy was entirely personal. She also said that Frank Sinatra later introduced her to Sam Giancana, with whom she also became intimate. She said that Giancana never asked her for any information related to Kennedy. She also said that John Roselli was her friend. In 1997, Exner alleged more details and changed her story, in separate interviews with Liz Smith of *Vanity Fair* and Seymour Hersh. She said Kennedy told her of his plans related to Cuba and used her to carry money to Giancana, as well as to arrange numerous meetings between him, Giancana, and Roselli. She claimed to Smith to have terminated a pregnancy resulting from the last encounter in

1962 with Kennedy. She said that she had carried payoffs from California defense contractors to the Kennedys, including Robert F. Kennedy. A witness of Hersh's who appeared to support Exner's story of carrying money to Giancana later dropped his story. Judith Campbell Exner lived in Newport Beach and was a painter. She died on September 24, 1999, in Duarte, California, from breast cancer.[9]

That's why the Giancana's, the family, has said that the murder was timed, intended to be entrapment of Bobby Kennedy. They were trying to solve two problems at once.

On the one hand, they had been asked to eliminate Marilyn Monroe because of the problems she presented to the CIA from her knowledge of classified things and concerned that she was getting ready to talk. On the other hand, because they had wiretaps, they knew that Bobby Kennedy was there that day. There's another reason they may have known he was there that afternoon too. Bobby Kennedy was staying at that time with a lawyer, who had been a lawyer for Sam Giancana. He represented the mob. He represented Sam Giancana during the Senate crime hearings. You can look at the old newsreels, and you'll see it's the same guy.

So, Bobby Kennedy was with him, and he takes off for Los Angeles. We don't know the extent of loyalties, disloyalty, treachery, who told what. We do know for sure that there were wiretaps, and the mob felt that, according to the Giancana family, if they struck then, the day after Bobby Kennedy had been there, then the police investigation would come up with his fingerprints. The investigation would show letters; maybe there would even be a diary. There would be things that would tie her to the Kennedys. The mob felt it would help bring the Kennedys down. That's what they wanted.

I agree with probably 95 percent of the Margolis book, except for their conclusion that Bobby Kennedy was actually involved with murdering her. I do not think that was the case.

Q. So, you said that not only did the CIA and FBI have Marilyn bugged, but Jimmy Hoffa did as well. Why would Hoffa have her house bugged?

A. That's a really good question. I have testimony from the wiretap guys, and one of them, Fred Otash, did the dirty work. He bugged her house when she was on a trip to Mexico. He also planted bugs at Peter Lawford's Malibu estate. Peter Lawford was a brother-in-law of JFK. They had big parties there. We think it may have been at one of those parties that JFK first met Marilyn Monroe. He was working on behalf of Hoffa and Sam Giancana. Hoffa was head of the teamsters, and they were deep in the mob's pockets as far as money. The early casinos were built in Las Vegas with heavy mob participation and the teamster's pension fund. I don't know if it was legal or illegal that the pension fund went into the hands of those who were building the casinos. So, they were all in bed together.

Fred Otash was a Los Angeles police officer, private investigator, author, and a WWII Marine veteran, who became known as a Hollywood fixer while operating as its most infamous private detective. He is most remembered as the inspiration for Jack Nicholson's character, Jake Gittes, in the film *Chinatown*. Otash worked for Hollywood Research Incorporated, which did business with the tabloid magazine *Confidential*. He was also known for being hired by Peter Lawford to investigate Marilyn Monroe. An FBI file released as part of the JFK Assassination Records suggests that Otash was investigating Lawford and John F. Kennedy and attempted to talk a call-girl into arranging a meeting with Kennedy in which she would wear a wire to record incriminating statements. Otash also was involved in the investigation of the "Wrong Door Raid" involving Frank Sinatra. Otash wrote about his life in his memoir, *Investigation Hollywood: Memoirs Of Hollywood's Top Private Detective*.[10]

Hoffa hated the Kennedys and Robert Kennedy as Attorney General. Same as Sam

Giancana. Once Marilyn became a sort of plaything of the Kennedys, first JFK and later Bobby, sure they wanted to wiretap her. They were looking for anything they could find to use against JFK and bring him down. In the end, they all got theirs. Jimmy Hoffa, you know he disappeared. Nobody found the body. In the case of Sam Giancana, it was eight bullets. Most of them to the head in his own home, assassinated. So, everybody got paid back in the end.

Q. There was a large fear of communism in America in the 1960s, and Marilyn actually had a tie to the communists as well, correct?

A. She walked right into the middle of it. First of all, let me say a little about Marilyn's background here. She was an orphan, her mother was still alive, but she grew up in an orphanage because her mother was psychologically incapable, and her mother was institutionalized. So, for all intents and purposes, she was an orphan. She went from foster home to foster home and was very, very poor. She had nothing in her early years, so she identified with under tribe. Some of the books she read were written by communists.

The other thing was she was very sympathetic to integration and the plight of the blacks. In those days in America, there was a big push in favor of integration and equal rights for blacks from the American Communist Party. The big point of departure for her was when she married Arthur Miller. He was a great playwright and wrote *Death of a Salesman*. You could say that he was either a communist, or he had communist leanings. In those days, there was a House on American Un-Activities Committee and Senator Joseph McCarthy and the witch hunt against any American citizens who had ties to the Communist Party, Russia, and Russian communism.

The House Un-American Activities Committee (HUAC) – from 1969 onwards, known as the House Committee on Internal Security, was an investigative committee of the United States

House of Representatives. The HUAC was created in 1938 to investigate alleged disloyalty and subversive activities on the part of private citizens, public employees, and those organizations suspected of having fascist or communist ties. The committee's anti-communist investigations are often compared to and confused with those of Joseph McCarthy, who, as a U.S. Senator, had no direct involvement with the House committee. McCarthy was the chairman of the Government Operations Committee and its Permanent Subcommittee on Investigations of the U.S. Senate, not the House.

In 1947, the committee held nine days of hearings into alleged communist propaganda and influence in the Hollywood motion picture industry. After conviction on contempt of Congress charges for refusal to answer some questions posed by committee members, "The Hollywood Ten" were blacklisted by the industry. Eventually, more than 300 artists, including directors, radio commentators, actors, and particularly screenwriters, were boycotted by the studios. Some, like Charlie Chaplin, Orson Welles, Alan Lomax, Paul Robeson, and Yip Harburg, left the U.S or went underground to find work. Others like Dalton Trumbo wrote under pseudonyms or the names of colleagues. Only about ten percent succeeded in rebuilding careers within the entertainment industry.

When the House abolished the committee in 1975, its functions were transferred to the House Judiciary Committee.[11]

> So, many people from Hollywood were called to testify in front of the House of Un-American Activities. Those who refused to name names, well, some of them went to jail. It was a crime not to cooperate with the committee. Arthur Miller, who had recently married Marilyn Monroe, at that point was called before the committee and was considered uncooperative. So, at that point, you had not only people like Hoffa and Giancana interested in wiretapping Marilyn Monroe but certainly the FBI. Especially so when she went to Mexico to visit a Vanderbilt heir, who was a communist. Then the CIA got involved in watching her, too, because the CIA's jurisdiction is espionage outside

the United States. She became a person of interest to all of these Government agencies, and she was in the thick of it but didn't know it. She really didn't know what deep water she was in. She was a bit naïve about it. It set up the circumstances where she became a serious target.

Q. Was her husband Arthur Miller blackballed from working too?

A. Good question. I know that the House of Un-American Activities censured him, which was really bad news but then they took it back. I don't know. He made some concessions. It was decided that he had not committed a criminal offense by refusing to give them whatever information that they wanted. He was not censured like other writers. One of his scripts called *The Misfits*, directed by John Huston, starred Marilyn Monroe, even though they were getting divorced at that time. They made his movie with his name on it. But there were other writers that couldn't work under their real names. They had to write all of their things anonymously. They would use a different name and get paid under the table. But her marriage to Arthur Miller was certainly a huge set back to her personal safety, if not her career.

"Playwright Arthur Miller defies the House Committee on Un-American Activities and refuses to name suspected communists."[12] When Miller attended the HUAC hearing, to which Monroe accompanied him, risking her own career, he gave the committee a detailed account of his political activities. Reneging on the chairman's promise, the committee demanded the names of friends and colleagues who had participated in similar activities. Miller refused to comply, saying, "I could not use the name of another person and bring trouble on him." As a result, a judge found Miller guilty of contempt of Congress in May 1957. Miller was sentenced to a fine and a prison sentence, blacklisted. His passport had already been denied when he tried to go to Brussels to attend the premiere of his play, *The Crucible*, about the Salem witch trials. In August 1958, his conviction was overturned by the court of appeals, which ruled that Miller had been misled by the chairman of the HUAC.[13]

Q. The last person to speak to Marilyn was Jose Bolanos?

A. Jose Bolanos claimed he was the last to talk with her. He has what I think is a very consistent story that held up, and he was extensively interviewed.

Jose Bolaños was born in Mexico City in 1935 and died there on June 11, 1994. He was known as something of a playboy but was also a screenwriter and director. He married Italian actress Venetia Vianello, but his biggest claim to fame is his relationship with Marilyn Monroe.[14]

But the mainstream people think that Peter Lawford was the last one to talk with her. Bolanos said that he had been her escort to the Golden Globes Awards that year. She had met him on a trip to Mexico. He was a Mexican screenwriter, quite handsome. He said that he was in Los Angeles that night and had called her. They were talking on the phone, and there had been some commotion at the door. She put down the phone and never returned. He said that something was going on in the background, that someone came in, and the phone just clicked.

The other key thing he said, I think, is that she said she knew a secret from the President that was so big it would change the whole world one day. He didn't ever admit if she did tell him what that secret was. But since he had that conversation, in an interview may have been with Donald Wolfe years later, you have to ask yourself what was that secret at that time in 1962, that would still have been secret by the time this interview happened.

That gets us to things like the "Roswell" case. I'm interested in that because, as you mentioned, I was the producer of Showtime's movie *Roswell* and the controversy about what happened in

Roswell in 1947. The military announced that they recovered a crashed flying saucer. Then they changed the story and said it was a weather balloon.

In the CIA document that I mentioned with James Angleton's signature, which we are really sure is a legitimate bonafide document for many reasons, it charted the contents of a wire conversation that Marilyn's friend Dorothy Kilgallen had with a Marilyn associate in New York. Some of the things that Marilyn had been told about by JFK came out in that wiretap. One of them was a visit to a secret airbase by John F. Kennedy for the purpose of examining things from outer space. It said that in the CIA document, and Dorothy Kilgallen speculated that it had to do with the downed flying saucer in that case, which would have been Roswell.

Dorothy Mae Kilgallen was an American journalist and television game show panelist. In 1938, she began her newspaper column, *The Voice of Broadway*, which eventually was syndicated to more than 140 papers. Kilgallen's columns featured mostly show business news and gossip but ventured into other topics, such as politics and organized crime. She wrote front-page articles on the Sam Sheppard trial and later the John F. Kennedy assassination. On November 8, 1965, Kilgallen was found dead in her Manhattan townhouse located at 45 East 68th Street. Her death was determined to have been caused by a fatal combination of alcohol and barbiturates. Several authors have claimed that she was murdered to prevent her from revealing a conspiracy to assassinate John F. Kennedy.[15]

Q. How do you feel about Roswell being the secret that Marilyn knew about because Kennedy told her?

A. Well, to make the movie *Roswell* I did extensive research, and I was involved with those who were doing great in-depth research at that time. One of them, Kevin Randle, who's just come out with a new book, *Roswell for the 21st Century*, has backed off in his certainty of it being extra-terrestrial.

I don't view kindly to what they call his recanting because I know some of the things he was told at that time, from, for example, the Provost Marshal, who was head of the Military Police that recovered the debris from the field. The debris that Intelligence Officer, Jessie Marcell, said in 1986, "Was not made on this Earth, and it couldn't have been."

I believe that all of the current theories are wrong. They are either deliberate disinformation or are mistaken. It was extra-terrestrial contact. There's so much good testimony from solid people about it who were there at that time.

I think because the Marilyn Monroe document, signed by the head of counterintelligence, mentions JFK's visit to a secret airbase for the purpose of examining things from outer space, I can agree with what Dorothy Kilgallen referred to as the downed flying saucer from outer space of the southwest in 1947.

I think all of these pieces historically interlock. One more point, how do we know that the CIA document is real? Some have said that it was a forgery. Well, no, it turns out that author Don Burleson went through the Freedom of Information Act procedures on that to look through the CIA transcripts of the wiretap referred to in that document. However, the first search by the CIA said that they hadn't found any transcripts. But you can appeal that if you want to. He appealed it through the proper procedures, and the CIA accepted his appeal of their original denial. He quite rightly pointed out that the CIA would have never accepted an appeal based on a document that was fraudulent or wasn't theirs.

Q. Most people believe that Marilyn died of an overdose either on purpose or by accident. How do you think that Marilyn died?

A. Well, the Giancana family claims that it was a suppository injection of the drugs she was taking. That jives with part of the autopsy report that talked about this purplish discoloration of the colon that was never satisfactorily explained. So, that's consistent.

The thing that isn't consistent with the idea that she swallowed a lot of pills was that no water glass was ever found in the room where her body was found. How did she take those pills? Some of the research indicated that the toxicity level of her blood was so high, so massive, that she would have died before taking that many pills. In other words, she would have been dead en route to get there in order for her blood toxicity to go there. There was none of the crystalline residue, usually found in cases like that, found in her stomach. Some researchers have tried to bring science into it and say, no, the stomach acids could have theoretically dissolved those capsules. Theoretically, it would have been possible, but they didn't see the residue.

The first policeman who came to the scene and discovered her, Sargent Jack Clemmons, was suspicious from the beginning saying, "It didn't look like a suicide. It looked like it was staged to look like a suicide." He has seen overdose victims before, and there was always vomit, but none in this case. The body is always contorted, but in this case, the body was just laid out perfectly as though it was posed.

Police Chief Tom Reddin said that it was handled like a top-secret intelligence operation in the hours after her death because of the Attorney General of the United States. I think what he meant was that it was kept secret to try to protect Bobby Kennedy. He was vulnerable in that situation. He was with her. He was in town, and he had an argument with her. They got him out of town. They spent five or six hours after her body was discovered before it was officially reported to Sargent Jack Clemmons, a low-level sergeant at the police department. But higher-level operatives had been working on cleaning up the scene for hours. That's why Marilyn looked staged to Sergeant Clemmons when he got there.

Bottom line – it was covered up. We were lied to. She didn't commit suicide. It was a contract killing. It was a terrible episode in American history. It's kind of presaged the violence that was to come. It was one year, approximately before the assassination of President Kennedy, that Marilyn was the result of a contract killing.

The first allegations that Marilyn had been murdered originated in anti-communist activist Frank A. Capell's self-published pamphlet, *The Strange Death of Marilyn Monroe 1964,* in which he claimed that her death was part of a communist conspiracy. He claimed that Monroe and U.S. Attorney General Robert F. Kennedy had an affair, which she took too seriously and was threatening to cause a scandal. Kennedy ordered her to be assassinated to protect his career. In addition to accusing Kennedy of being a communist sympathizer, Capell also claimed that many other people close to Monroe, such as her doctors and ex-husband Arthur Miller, were communists. Capell's credibility has been seriously questioned because his only source was columnist Walter

Winchell, who in turn had received much of his information from Capell, therefore, was citing himself.

His friend, LAPD Sergeant Jack Clemmons, aided him in developing his pamphlet. Clemmons became a central source for conspiracy theorists. He was the first Police Officer on the scene of Monroe's death and later made claims that he had not mentioned in the official 1962 investigation that when he arrived at Monroe's house, her housekeeper was washing her sheets, and he had a sixth sense that something was wrong.

Capell and Clemmons' allegations have been linked to their political goals. Capell dedicated his life to revealing an "International Communist Conspiracy," and Clemmons was a member of The Police and Fire Research Organization (FiPo), which sought to expose "subversive activities which threaten our American way of life." FiPo and similar organizations were known for their stance against the Kennedys and for sending the Federal Bureau of Investigation letters incriminating them. The 1964 FBI file that speculated on an affair between Monroe and

Robert F. Kennedy is likely to have come from them.

Furthermore, Capell, Clemmons, and a third person were indicted in 1965 by a California grand jury for conspiracy to libel by obtaining and distributing a false affidavit. They claimed that Senator Thomas Kuchel had once been arrested for a homosexual act. They had done this because Kuchel had supported the Civil Rights Act of 1964. Capell pleaded guilty, and charges against Clemmons were dropped after he resigned from the LAPD.[16]

Listen to the full interview with Paul Davids on my website:

houseofmysteryradio/episodes/paul-davids-marilyn-declassified

1. *Marilyn Monroe: Declassified* | Online Video | SBS Movies. https://www.sbs.com.au/movies/video/869149251582/Marilyn-Monroe-Declassified
2. https://en.wikipedia.org/wiki/Thomas_Reddin

3. https://en.wikipedia.org/wiki/Daryl_Gates
4. https://en.wikipedia.org/wiki/Sam_Giancana
5. https://www.simonandschuster.com/books/Double-Cross/Sam-Giancana/9781510711259
6. https://en.wikipedia.org/wiki/Rafael_Trujillo
7. https://en.wikipedia.org/wiki/James_Jesus_Angleton
8. https://en.wikipedia.org/wiki/Mary_Pinchot_Meyer
9. https://en.wikipedia.org/wiki/Judith_Exner
10. https://en.wikipedia.org/wiki/Fred_Otash
11. https://en.wikipedia.org/wiki/House_Un-American_Activities_Committee
12. https://www.history.com/this-day-in-history/arthur-miller-refuses-to-name-communists
13. https://www.litlovers.com/reading-guides/fiction/8674-death-of-a-salesman-miller?start=1
14. https://www.imdb.com/name/nm0049443/bio?ref_=nm_ov_bio_sm
15. https://en.wikipedia.org/wiki/Dorothy_Kilgallen
16. https://en.wikipedia.org/wiki/Death_of_Marilyn_Monroe

Case Closed

INTERVIEW WITH JAY MARGOLIS & RICHARD BUSKIN

New York Times bestselling authors Jay Margolis and Richard Buskin co-authored *The Murder of Marilyn Monroe: Case Closed*. On October 15, 2014, The National Press Club in Washington, D.C. accepted Margolis and Buskin's book for display at the 37th Annual Book Fair & Authors' Night, in partnership with Politics & Prose. *The Murder of Marilyn Monroe: Case Closed* was translated into Italian, French, and Russian and became a New York Times Bestseller. On October 27, 2014, the bestselling authors appeared in the United Kingdom documentary, directed by Renny Bartlett and entitled *The Missing Evidence: The Death of

Marilyn Monroe, a Blink Films production in association with the Smithsonian Channel.

Margolis graduated summa cum laude from the University of Southern California and became a Jesse Unruh Research Scholar for his paper on African American Reparations. Richard Buskin is a New York Times bestselling author and freelance journalist specializing in film, music, television, and pop culture. His articles have appeared in newspapers and magazines worldwide, and among the thirty nonfiction books he has written are biographies of Marilyn Monroe, Princess Diana, Whitney Houston, and Sheryl Crow. A native of London, England, he lives in Chicago, Illinois.

Q. What started you guys on the *Murder of Marilyn Monroe: Case Closed* book that you wrote together?

RBA. Around 1993, I started a book about the films of Marilyn Monroe. The whole idea was that there were so many books about her life, affairs, and her death, so how about doing a book about her career.

No one had really done one in-depth. I did that book. It took me a few years to research and write it, and it ended up coming out in 2001. It was called *Blonde Heat: The Sizzling Screen Career of Marilyn Monroe*.

During the course of doing that book, people were constantly asking me what my theory was about her death. It was amazing, no matter how much I was focusing on the film career, the way that Marilyn died, the circumstances, and the mystery surrounding it, was clearly what was fascinating people. When I hooked up with Jay, he was focusing on that aspect of her life. He had already done so much research; it was stunning what he had come up with. For me, it was really a compelling subject to write a book about.

JMA. The first book I had ever picked up about Marilyn Monroe was by George Barris. He believed that she was murdered, and he wrote that in his book. Everybody had these three different camps. There was either murder, suicide, or accident. These were the three main arguments that people believed in. I thought that seemed pretty unresolved, so I thought I'd like to investigate it, which led me to believe she was murdered with an empty stomach.

I thought it was pretty unique that at the time of her death, she was the most famous woman in the world, and nobody else had ever done that at that time. Now we have something different. In today's age, we have Instagram, where anybody can get a million followers if they really know what they're doing. So, it's not the same. It's a different time, and things have changed. But at the time of her death, there was no internet. So, for her to become that, was nothing short of remarkable – to become the most famous woman in the world.

RBA. She was really a self-made woman swimming against the tide of the Hollywood studio system, which was run by men. Over the course of her career, she really came up with that breathy, dumb blondes, Marilyn persona that everyone knows and loves. But then she also went on to become a serious actress. She had intense coaching under several top drama coaches and formed her own production company with her choice of director, scripts, and even costars. This is someone who really came from nothing and made herself into the icon that she became.

Q. She was probably the biggest star at the time of her death, I would imagine. Elizabeth Taylor was doing quite well then too, but Monroe was probably the big box office at the time, correct?

RBA. Yes, she was. Liz Taylor was commanding a million dollars for *Cleopatra*, which was more than Marilyn was getting. But one of the things that had been incorrectly reported over the years was that Marilyn died in disgrace. Her career was in the doldrums, and she was fired from her last film. What wasn't known at the time and only came out over the years is that in her last film, when she was fired from it, they tried to replace Marilyn in the film, *Something's got to Give*. But her costar, Dean Martin, refused to work with anybody but

Marilyn. So, they ended up having to go back to her and upping her salary from $100,000 to half a million dollars, with a contract for a second film for the same fee. So, her career was actually on the rise, and not the downward spiral when she died.

Q. Why did the studio keep it quiet about them rehiring Marilyn?

RBA. It was very convenient for the studio. They rehired her just before her death. They hadn't announced it yet because it was going to put egg on their faces, but she died in the meantime. So, they didn't have to. They just left it like that. The general public never knew what the backstory was.

Q. Do you think the studio had anything to do with her death?

JMA. No, not directly. They had a lot to do with the cover-up after her death. Once they were notified, they took the documents that promised to rehire her, and they did a whole cleanup job of anything that was to their benefit.

Q. You were saying earlier that Marilyn put on that dumb persona, and she was quite different from how people perceived her.

RBA. Yes, she was. A, she was way more intelligent than not only how the general public perceived her, but certainly how the studio bosses did. She rose through the ranks from a starlet to a superstar based on the breathy, dumb blonde persona. That was cash at the box office for Twentieth Century Fox, and they didn't want to meddle with that formula. So, when she established herself and said that she wanted to become serious and wanted to be cast in a film like *The Brothers Karamazov*, they laughed at her. They said, "Are you kidding? You're not capable of that, and we're not interested."

The Brothers Karamazov was a 1958 film made by MGM, based on Fyodor Dostoevsky's 1880 novel *The Brothers Karamazov*. It was directed by Richard Brooks and produced by Pandro S. Berman. The screenplay was by Julius J. Epstein, Philip G. Epstein, and Richard Brooks. It was entered into the 1958 Cannes Film Festival. The brothers were played by Yul Brynner, Richard Basehart, and William Shatner in his film debut.

Marilyn Monroe was rumored to be in negotiations to play the role of Grushenka, but several conflicting accounts arose around the time the film entered production. An MGM executive said she'd turned down the role in part because she was expecting a baby, but Monroe's agent denied this and claimed that the studio had never even made her an offer. Richard Brooks said that Monroe would have made a fine Grushenka but claimed negotiations fell through because of her contractual demands and personal troubles.[1]

> That's the point in which she walked out on the contract. It was after she completed the *Seven Year Itch*. She walked out, went to New York for a year, and studied under Lee Strasberg. She refused to return until it was under her terms.

Lee Strasberg was a Polish-born American actor, director, and theatre practitioner. He co-founded, with directors Harold Clurman and Cheryl Crawford, the Group Theatre in 1931, which was hailed as America's first true theatrical collective. In 1951, he became director of the nonprofit Actors Studio in New York City, considered the nation's most prestigious acting school. In 1966, he was involved in the creation of Actors Studio West in Los Angeles.

Although other highly regarded teachers also developed "The Method," Strasberg is often considered the "Father of Method Acting in America," according to author Mel Gussow, and from the 1920s until his death in 1982, "he revolutionized the art of acting by having a profound influence on performance in American theater and film." From his base in New York, he trained several generations of theatre and film notables, including Anne Bancroft, Dustin Hoffman, Montgomery Clift, James Dean, Marilyn Monroe, Jane Fonda, Julie Harris, Paul Newman, Ellen Burstyn, Al Pacino, Robert De Niro, Geraldine Page, Eli Wallach, and directors Frank Perry and Elia Kazan.[2]

Q. What was her marital state at the time?

JMA. At the time of *Something's got to Give*, she wasn't married. She had already divorced Arthur Miller.

Q. So, after she was divorced from Arthur Miller, I heard there were rumors that she was going to remarry Joe DiMaggio?

JMA. That is correct. In statements made by her half-sister, Berniece Miracle, and niece, Mona Rae Miracle, they both affirmed that she was going to remarry Joe DiMaggio. In fact, Mona Rae said, according to Berniece, Marilyn was looking forward to it, and it was definitely going to happen. The executor of Joe DiMaggio's estate, Morris Engelberg, said the date was set for August 8, 1962, which was the date that they actually had her funeral.

Q. Did DiMaggio admit to their upcoming marriage at all?

JMA. No. He was always notoriously tight-lipped about anything involving the relationship between him and Marilyn Monroe. He did this out of respect for her.

He didn't want anything about his relationship with her to be exploited. So, he never said a word about anything.

Q. Let's talk about her drug use. The press has said that she was using a lot of drugs, alcohol, and sleeping pills. What did you find out about her drug use?

JMA. She was not worse than any other person who was given pills at the studio. She did get addicted to sleeping pills towards the end, and her psychiatrist, Doctor Greenson, claimed he was concerned. He was allegedly trying to wean her off of sleeping pills, along with her physician Dr. Hyman Engelberg. He claimed that instead of her taking Nembutal she would often take, he had her take Chloral Hydrate. Dr. Engelberg said he never prescribed it, but if you look at the prescription he wrote on June 7, 1962, one day before she got fired from *Something's got to Give*, it's very clear he prescribed Choral Hydrate. So, he lied when he said that Marilyn must have got it from Tijuana. As far as dependency, she was not an alcoholic.

She may have had her Dom Perignon Champagne, which she loved a lot, but she was not drinking every day.

Q. Why did her personal doctor lie?

JMA. I think Engelberg lied because he realized it was an awful lot of prescriptions to be prescribed at the same time, and people might not understand if it was true that he was trying to wean her off of these pills. There were 15 different kinds of pill bottles on her bed-stand at the time she died. That's an awful lot of pills, and he probably didn't want to say he prescribed all of them. So, he was definitely covering for himself.

Q. What can you tell us about JFK and Marilyn?

RBA. I can tell you that the JFK and Marilyn affair very likely started up in the 1950s, long before he was president actually. He suffered from severe back problems, and there was one occasion in the mid-fifties where he was in the hospital, and one of the people who visited him reported there was a portrait of Marilyn on his bedside table in the hospital room. So, it's very likely that it started that early.

Q. So, you don't think that they were having an affair at the time of her death?

JMA. At the time of her death, she had switched over to Bobby Kennedy. Fred Otash, who bugged her house and Peter Lawford's house, noticed from all of the tapes he listened to that there were apparently now more tapes from her and Bobby, as opposed to Jack and Marilyn.

Files belonging to private investigator Fred Otash claimed that both President John F. Kennedy and his brother Bobby, the nation's Attorney General during the early 1960s, had a sexual relationship with actress Marilyn Monroe according to *The Hollywood Reporter*. The documents were discovered by Colleen Otash, the daughter of the private investigator who died in 1992. The famed Hollywood private investigator also claimed to have listened to Marilyn Monroe die after a violent argument with the Kennedys through a bug he installed in her Los Angeles home. It was only later that Fred Otash claimed to have learned that Marilyn Monroe had died following the argument he recorded on August 5, 1962.

Otash had worked for Hollywood Research Incorporated, which did investigate work for the notorious gossip magazine of that day, *Confidential*. Fred Otash claimed that he had recorded President Kennedy and Marilyn Monroe having sex after bugging the home of the Kennedys brother-in-law and actor, Peter Lawford.

It is important to note that according to White House records from the Kennedy administration, on the day that Marilyn Monroe died, President and Mrs. Kennedy were both vacationing in Hyannis Port, Massachusetts. The Kennedy family went to Catholic mass, visited the homes of the Shrivers, and Ted Kennedy, as well the first family, went sailing. However, the records from the White House give no indication of Bobby Kennedy's whereabouts.[3]

So, she had switched over from sleeping with John F. Kennedy, which is a well-documented case from March 24th to March 26th at Bing Crosby's house in Palm Springs. It's very well accepted by almost every Marilyn biographer that there was a tryst there. Ralph Roberts, her trusted masseur, told Marilyn biographers, and nobody ever doubted him that she did sleep with the president on that date.

Another trusted friend, Sydney Guilaroff, her hairstylist since the *Asphalt Jungle* in the 1950s, also relayed in his own book that on the last day of her life, Marilyn called him about 2:30 p.m. and said that Bobby Kennedy and Peter Lawford had just left her house. She told him in confidence that she was sleeping with JFK and also sleeping with Robert Kennedy. And that everything had gone wrong. She was worried, and she didn't tell a lot of people that she had affairs with both the Kennedy brothers.

Sydney Guilaroff was the "Hairdresser to the Stars." The man who created some of the most lasting and legendary styles during Hollywood's Golden Age also was one of the most incredible confidants celebrities had ever whispered to. The guiding force in Guilaroff's rise to prominence as "Hairdresser to the Stars" was effectuated by actress Joan Crawford. Crawford brought Guilaroff to Hollywood and MGM, where he held the position of chief hairstylist from 1934 into the late 1970s. At a time when a star's screen appearance was a significant function of the studio's image machine, Guilaroff's skills crafted distinctive looks, which came to be identifiable with the stars for which they were conceived. He was recognized as a master in his profession with an instinctive, creative eye. Guilaroff gave Claudette Colbert her bangs, made Lucille Ball a redhead, gave Judy Garland her *Wizard of Oz* braids, and cut, curled, coiffed, and cosseted virtually every other MGM star in his 40-year reign as Hollywood's most creative and celebrated hairdresser.[4] Guilaroff maintained his most formidable undertaking had been his work for the 1938 film *Marie Antoinette*, for which 2,000 court wigs were required and an additional 3,000 wigs for the extra players. Grace Kelly chose Guilaroff to style her hair for her 1956 wedding to Prince Rainier of Monaco.

But she had told Guilaroff that she had threatened Bobby she was going to go public. Bobby's response, according to Marilyn, was to say, "If you threaten me, Marilyn, there's more than one way to keep you quiet." It was at that point Bobby left, and she called Guilaroff. She was hysterical and crying while she was on the phone with him, relaying all of this information.

Q. We had another guest on the show earlier that said she was pregnant at the time of her death as well?

JMA. No, that is not true.

Q. But you think that she was having an affair with both Kennedys in August just before she died?

JMA. Marilyn was actually alternating between JFK and Bobby Kennedy. A lot of people thought that once she had finished with Jack, it was on to Bobby. But according to John Danoff, and what he heard, there were instances where she would go off with Bobby, and then back to John again.

The Last Days of Marilyn Monroe is a documentary that includes an interview with a private detective, John Danoff, who claims that at the behest of an unnamed client, he once listened through a bugging device to lovemaking between Monroe and President John F. Kennedy. The incident was said to have occurred at the home of the late actor Peter Lawford, who was married to Patricia Kennedy, sister of the late president.[5]

Q. So, you are eliminating the suicide reason for her death?

JMA. There's absolutely no way she committed suicide, and there's a number of compelling reasons for this. She couldn't have had enough drugs to match the amount that was in her blood. She didn't have the pills to match the drugs found in her blood. She would have needed 47 Nembutals, but she had a prescription for 25 Nembutals on July 25, 1962. She got a refill of 25 pills on August 3, 1962. So, that's a total of 50. Ralph Roberts researched and discovered that she took about 6 Nembutals a day. So, for her to have that many on hand, it would assume that she waited and had not taken those six pills per day in order to take the 47 that killed her. That's really not logical. Also, the fact that she had no pills in her stomach, and she was purported to have 64 pills. So, where did 64 pills go from her stomach?

RBA. Another thing is that there are photos of the death-scene shot by the police, and you can see pill bottles on the bedside table with the caps screwed back on. Someone in that state, shoving pills down their throat at that rate, would they take the time to meticulously put the caps back on these empty bottles and just line them up on the table? It was a staged scene.

Q. What did the coroner say happened to her?

JMA. The coroner did a really strange thing. She was murdered on August 4, 1962. Her body was discovered dead on the 5th. Then, on the 18th, he gave a public press conference where he said, "It is our opinion that it is probably suicide." He said that "it is our opinion." He did not say that it was definitive.

He just caused more and more speculation, which was really suspicious because he asserted that she would have had to swallow 47 Nembutals and a large amount of Chloral Hydrate. Yet, Dr. Noguchi has always said it was suicide, but over the years, when you see him on camera, like on *History Mysteries*, he will say stuff like, "The coroner's office tried to prove suicide, but they couldn't show any factors that would lead to suicide." So, he's actually playing around it without diverting from the initial findings. But you can tell that there's more than what he's saying.

Q. You said she had been bugged and that there were people listening to her?

JMA. Yes. I spoke with the sound man that went with Fred Otash the night she died, and he was responsible for listening to those tapes. He said that Bobby and Marilyn were sleeping together, and yes, John F. Kennedy and Marilyn were sleeping together, from what he heard on the tapes. He's the one that was listening to them. He was the one that took them out on orders by the Kennedys. Fred Otash had many different clients, and he was working for Jimmy Hoffa when the bugs were installed. He noticed that there were other bugs installed when he was putting them in there. So, there were many different people listening in. There was the FBI, CIA, Jimmy Hoffa, at one point even Howard Hughes, according to Otash. So, many different clients were listening in on what Marilyn was doing.

RBA. J. Edgar Hoover was no fan of the Kennedys. So, any evidence they (the FBI) could get on their indiscretions was gold dust to him. So, as Jay says, there were many invested interests in this.

Q. What can you tell us about her last day?

JMA. Well, she threatened to hold a press conference when Bobby Kennedy came to her house and told her that she couldn't see him or Jack, and they no longer wanted her to write or call anymore. I've always found it suspicious that once I discovered Bobby Kennedy was at her house, all of a sudden, she just has a lethal amount of drugs in her body. Just a few hours later. Is that just some sort of strange coincidence? I don't think so.

The two events are connected. This is totally scary. You know how a man like Bobby Kennedy can attempt to hide his presence at her house, and then say he was at John Bates' ranch near San Francisco. How could he do that unless he had these absolutely powerful resources to cover up every one of his tracks. But that's exactly what he did. There are more than 20 witnesses who saw him there. So, he can't deny it.

Q. So, you are putting him behind the murder then?

JMA. Yes, he was the one that made it happen.

Q. Who else was involved?

JMA. Ralph Greenson, the psychiatrist who stuck a heart needle into her chest. He tried to play it off for any witnesses, including the ambulance attendants who were witnessing it, that it was adrenaline. But it wasn't. James Hall, the ambulance attendant, always said that it was a brownish fluid. So, it was an undiluted Pentobarbital injection to the heart.

Pentobarbital is a short-acting barbiturate typically used as a sedative, a pre-anesthetic, and to control convulsions in emergencies. It can also be used for short-term treatment of insomnia but has been largely replaced by the benzodiazepine family of drugs.[6]

Also, according to James Hall, Greenson said not to make a show of this. So, Greenson was trying to make it look like he was trying to help her, but he was really trying to kill her. So, he sticks it into her heart, and there were five eyewitnesses. There's the two attendants, James Hall and Murray Liebowitz. Murray Liebowitz told Donald Wolf in 1993 that James Hall was telling the truth. Then, Peter Lawford confirmed the two attendants by stating, "Marilyn has got to be silenced," as he told Ralph Greenson. The reason Greenson had the motive to do this is, A, he's sick and tired of his patient. He constantly complained that he had to deal with her six or seven times a week when she was calling him up. But the thing that put him over the top was that Bobby Kennedy tricked him. Bobby told him that not only was she going to go public on Monday morning, August 6th, with this press conference exposing him and Jack, but she was going to go and expose him too with their affair they had. So, Bobby used Greenson to get rid of Marilyn. Bobby convinced the psychiatrist that Marilyn would also go public about the psychiatrist. But, in reality, Marilyn was only going to go public with Bobby and Jack.

Ralph R. Greenson was a prominent American psychiatrist and psychoanalyst. Greenson is famous for being Marilyn Monroe's psychiatrist and was the basis for Leo Rosten's 1963 novel, *Captain Newman, M.D.* The book was later made into a movie starring Gregory Peck as Greenson's character. There has been much conjecture by investigating officers, the press, and the public about Greenson's involvement in a possible cover-up concerning the circumstances of Monroe's death.

Q. So, Marilyn was having an affair with Greenson as well.

JMA. Yes, Marilyn was sleeping with Greenson too.

RBA. And for Greenson, a psychiatrist, not only was he married, but that went against professional ethics and would get him disbarred.

Q. Did Greenson ever talk about the murder?

JMA. Yes, Greenson did a very strange thing. Roy Turner, Marilyn's genealogist, once wrote to Greenson in eighth grade because he was doing a book report about Marilyn and asked him how Marilyn died. Greenson wrote him back and said that he wanted to make it very clear that she did not commit suicide. That goes against the official verdict. So, it's very strange how he kept hinting that she didn't commit suicide. He did love his patients, and he did felt bitter after realizing that Bobby Kennedy tricked him. Perhaps he may not have gone through with it, even though he was sick of his patient.

Q. Did anybody talk with her on her last day alive? Was her mood good, or was she depressed? Do we have any idea?

JMA. Yes, Gloria Romanoff said that on the evening she was found, August 5th, she had a dinner engagement that Frank Sinatra and her. Romanoff said that Marilyn was so happy about going that she was trying to figure out what dress she should wear. She was so focused on attending that dinner engagement, so why would she kill herself?

Ralph Roberts said that the last weekend she was the happiest that he had seen her in quite some time. He made a statement himself that he thought somebody had done her in. Roberts called Marilyn on August 4th at 6 p.m., trying to confirm a dinner engagement that he and Marilyn had. Greenson answered the phone and told him that Marilyn was not there. He was quite rude and hung up on him. Ralph Roberts thought that was very suspicious, and he doesn't believe the verdict. He is one of her friends that believes she was murdered.

RBA. A number of people I spoke with, and you have to bear in mind that people can express they feel great to friends and loved ones and still kill themselves. They may be hiding something, or their mind may just flip on them. But there was an overwhelming number of people who even told me during the course of researching my original *Blonde Heat* book that she seemed happy that last week of her life.

The story has always been that she was really depressed about the end of the relationship with the Kennedys. In fact, her stand-in on her final three movies, Evelyn Moriarty, said that she spoke with Marilyn a couple of nights before she died. Marilyn was upbeat because she had won the battle with Twentieth Century Fox, and she couldn't wait to get back to work. She was phoning members of the cast and crew, really excited and looking forward to what was coming up for her. So, that is not definitive evidence that she did not commit suicide, but it's a contributing piece of evidence.

Q. Did Marilyn ever attempt suicide before?

JMA. Yes, she did. There were maybe a half-a-dozen times when she attempted suicide before. One of the times was when she was dropped from Columbia Pictures. She wanted to be the best, and that was very discouraging for her, so she attempted to take her life then. Arthur Miller can also attest to a time. But that was at a time in her life when she felt discouraged. But she had more strength later on. She had gotten more confident being an actress.

RBA. The fact that she had attempted suicide, had a sleeping pill problem, and enjoyed Dom Perignon really helped with the stories that she killed herself. She was irresponsible. She was a wreck of a human being and wanted to die.

Q. Do you think that this murder was premeditated, down to the day and time, or do you think that it just happened?

JMA. I think that everything led to another part of it happening. It was not something that was completely planned. There was one thing that was for sure. Bobby Kennedy could not find that red diary of Marilyn's the night she died. So, they had to go to Plan B. Bobby called up the psychiatrist Greenson and told him he had to do it because Marilyn was going public about his affair with her.

Q. Did the witnesses, such as the ambulance attendant, James Hall, not think there was something strange going on when they saw the psychiatrist jabbing a needle into Marilyn's heart?

JMA. Yes, here's the thing, James Hall said that there was nothing sinister at the time he witnessed this. He thought it was adrenaline and that he was trying to save her. But it failed. He said that there was something very strange when he started to smell her mouth and there was no odor of pear. So, there was no way she could have swallowed those Chloral Hydrate pills. He also noticed that there was no indication of vomit. Most people who take a lot of drugs vomit the pills up. There was no indication of vomit. He said that she was still alive and that she was still breathing, but just barely.

So, he tried to get her off the bed and onto the floor so they could give her CPR. Her color started to come back. Then, all of a sudden, Greenson pushes him aside and said to give her positive pressure. Greenson pulled out of his little green medical bag, and a syringe with a heart needle was already affixed to it. He then said that they have to insert it between the ribs. Then, he inserted it into her heart. He then pronounced her dead after a few minutes.

James Hall thought that this was strange, and that if he had not come in there, he could have taken her to the hospital. But it wasn't until 20 years later, when they did a serious investigation of the case, that he learned for the first time that the autopsy report said that there were no pills in her stomach. Then, he said, "Now I kind of question what I saw." He always mentioned it was a brown fluid, and so that's not adrenaline.

Q. If there was nothing in her stomach, didn't that bring up questions?

JMA. Yes, absolutely, because there were enough drugs in her blood to kill three people. There was 4.5 mg percent of Nembutal in her blood, which is equivalent to 47 Nembutal. Then, there was 8 mg percent of Chloral Hydrate in her blood, which is equivalent to 17 Chloral Hydrate. That's about 64 pills. And yet Noguchi said, "I didn't find any refractile crystals from the Nembutal, and I didn't find any refractile crystals of the Chloral Hydrate."

Thomas Noguchi, in 1967, became Chief Medical Examiner-Coroner for the County of Los Angeles. As CME, Noguchi came to public attention for a series of autopsies which he performed or supervised on a range of celebrities and public figures that included Albert Dekker, Robert F. Kennedy, Sharon Tate, Janis Joplin, Inger Stevens, Gia Scala, David Janssen, William Holden, Natalie Wood, Marilyn Monroe, and John Belushi.[7]

Yet, in all of the competent medical professionals that you interview, they will tell you that there should have been undissolved capsules. So, what that means is that she didn't swallow the drugs that killed her.

Q. Could something like this happen today?

JMA. No, there's no way this could have happened today. Something would have been on YouTube in a matter of minutes. Somebody would have captured something on their iPhone. Actually, Mary W. Goodykoontz Barnes, Marilyn's neighbor, saw Bobby Kennedy and his two bodyguards, Archie Case and James Aher, go in there. If she had an iPhone, she would have captured them on camera. This was back in 1962, and we didn't have any of that. The principals at the scene were able to control the scene by having all of their people cover it up.

Q. You were able to talk to her neighbors then?

JMA. Mary W. Goodykoontz Barnes died in 1964, but she talked to Sgt. Jack Clemens in 1962, days after Marilyn's death. She didn't give her name to Clemens, and it's not on the deed to her house, which is sealed from the public until 2039. The reason we found out, and it was the first time in all of the books written on Marilyn Monroe, was that Joan Greenson wrote Goodykoontz Barnes' name in her manuscript.

So, we now know who the neighbor was that spoke to Sgt. Clemens. Clemens relayed that Barnes saw Bobby Kennedy and his two guards go into Marilyn's house on the last night of her life. We also have statements from neighbors Abe and Ruby Landau, who assert that there was an ambulance around midnight, and that's when they got home from their dinner party.

Listen to the full interview on my website:

houseofmysteryradio/episodes/marlyn-monroe-jay-margolis-richard-buskin

---

1. *The Brothers Karamazov* (1958 film) - Wikipedia. https://en.wikipedia.org/wiki/The_Brothers_Karamazov_(1958_film)
2. Lee Strasberg Movies - scripts. https://www.scripts.com/actor/lee_strasberg
3. Private Investigator: "I listened to Marilyn Monroe die." http://www.digitaljournal.com/article/351945
4. Sydney Guilaroff - Wikipedia. https://en.wikipedia.org/wiki/Sydney_Guilaroff
5. "RFK Ended Affair With Marilyn Day She Died," ex-maid Says https://www.sun-sentinel.com/news/fl-xpm-1985-10-07-8502130427-story.html
6. Pentobarbital - Wikipedia. https://en.wikipedia.org/wiki/Pentobarbital
7. Thomas Noguchi - Wikipedia. https://en.wikipedia.org/wiki/Thomas_Noguchi

PART III
Bob Crane

Hogan's Heroes debuted on CBS in the fall of 1965, and it was an overnight hit. Very loosely inspired by the 1963 World War II movie, *The Great Escape*, it featured a group of inmates in a German prisoner-of-war camp outsmarting a remarkably inept German army for six seasons.

Actor Bob Crane starred as Colonel Robert E. Hogan, coordinating an international crew of Allied prisoners running a special operations group from the camp. Werner Klemperer played Colonel Wilhelm Klink, the gullible commandant of the camp, and John Banner played the blundering but lovable sergeant-of-the-guard, Hans Schultz.[1]

Before going in front of the camera, the Connecticut-born Bob Crane made his name as a radio host, interviewing Marilyn Monroe, Bob Hope, and Charlton Heston on CBS' L.A. flagship station, KNX. After TV writer Carl Reiner appeared on Crane's radio show, he gave the broadcaster a guest gig as a philandering husband on *The Dick Van Dyke Show*. That led to a regular spot as a happy-go-lucky dentist on *The Donna Reed Show*.[2]

When I was just a kid back in the early 1960s, one of the many popular television shows I'd like to watch was *Hogan's Heroes*. But quite often, I wasn't allowed to watch as my father thought it was a disgrace that it made fun of the war, and it made it look like it was easy to beat the "stupid Germans." Of course, none of this was true. There was no way I could understand his feelings since I wasn't alive during the war and knew nobody that was in it. I was only between the age of three to nine when the show aired. But for him, his father, and many of his friends and their fathers, they knew the gravity of the war. And they knew many people who were in it and many who were killed.

I was a big-time radio kid. I loved old-time radio shows like the classic, *Suspense*, or the most popular, *The Shadow*, but even if there wasn't a great crime show on. I listened to radio, and this is how I come to know Bob Crane, as a radio DJ. In 1956, Crane was hired by CBS Radio to host the morning show at its West Coast flagship KNX in Los Angeles, California, partly to re-energize that station's ratings – he played jazz music and was funny. I'd say that he was the first one to try to do something different with radio, almost like Howard Stern but because it was in the fifties, much tamer!

The Murder

In the wealthy suburb of Phoenix, Arizona, Scottsdale was full of luxury resorts in what Arizonans call the "Valley of the Sun." June 29, 1978, likely began as nearly all Scottsdale summer days do with temperatures soaring above 100 degrees by high noon and the residents taking refuge in an air-conditioned bar in the town.

The police got a call from one of the city's apartment complexes about a murder. When they entered the dark first-floor apartment, they found the naked and battered body of a 49-year-old man, sprawled in his bed with two huge gashes above his left ear and an electrical cord knotted around his neck. He looked to be in good shape and had salt-and-pepper hair, but it was hard to identify him. There was so much blood splattered over the wall and ceiling apartment, and his pillow was red.

After learning that the apartment was leased to the nearby Windmill Dinner Theatre, the police asked the theatre's manager, Ed Beck, to identify the corpse. "There was no way I could identify him from one side," Beck told the press. "The other side, yes."

The bludgeoned form had once been Bob Crane, a TV star known to millions as the wise-cracking title character on the 1960s sitcom *Hogan's Heroes*. Crane's grisly murder revealed he had been doing a very different sort of on-camera work behind closed doors.

Four decades later, the still-unsolved slayings of the enigmatic actor with its links to the world of sex addiction and pornography has spawned a 2002 movie, at least five books, three investigations, and a vast spider's web of speculation.[3]

---

1. https://en.wikipedia.org/wiki/Hogan%27s_Heroes
2. https://ew.com/tv/2019/08/26/bob-crane-hogans-heroes-unsolved-murder/
3. https://ew.com/tv/2019/08/26/bob-crane-hogans-heroes-unsolved-murder/

DNA

INTERVIEW WITH JOHN HOOK

John Hook has been covering Arizona news for 36 years. He began his broadcast career in Phoenix radio. Prior to joining FOX 10, he was an anchor and reporter for eight years in Tucson. John has covered 12 National Political Conventions, the elections of six Presidents, and major breaking stories from the San Francisco earthquake to the OJ Simpson trial, to the California wildfires, and 9/11.

John holds a Bachelor of Arts in broadcasting from Arizona State University. In 2002, he was inducted into the Hall of Fame at ASU's Walter Cronkite School of Journalism.[1]

John Hook's interview for his book, *Who killed Bob Crane The Final Close-up?* took place in the summer of 2017.

Q. What brought you into the Bob Crane murder case?

A. When I headed off to college, Arizona State University, I ended up down here in the summer of 1978. I happen to get here a month after Bob Crane was murdered in his apartment in Scottsdale. My dorm in Arizona State was a mere seven miles away from where Bob Crane was murdered.

Then, the trial of John Carpenter, which we will get into that later, but John Carpenter went on trial in 1994, shortly after I arrived at Channel 10 in Phoenix Fox 10. He went on trial, but that trial was smothered out by another trial at the time, the OJ Simpson trial, which I did cover. So, I wasn't paying a lot of attention to the trial of Crane and it kind of vanished in the haze of OJ Simpson. It got lost a little bit in the shuffle, and I think it would have been high profile if that had not occurred at the same time.

Then I interviewed Bob Crane's son, Bob Jr., who wrote the foreword for my book, *Who Killed Bob Crane,* in March of 2015. At the conclusion of the interview, I was just struck by a guy who is now in his sixties, who every day still feels the pain and loss of his father, who he was very close to. The two were actually sharing an apartment back in California when Bob Crane wasn't out on the road. They were living together when he was murdered. I just felt that loss and thought that it was so terribly unfair that the family still had no definitive answers as to who killed Bob Crane.

I can't tell you how it came to me. It was kind of an "aha" moment, but is that evidence from the case still around, the blood evidence? If we found it, could we possibly retest it and get a definitive answer using DNA science, modern DNA science about who killed Bob Crane? That's how I started on this path.

That's when I called Bob Crane Jr. and told him I had an idea. He said, "What have you got?" I told him that I wanted to try and find the original DNA in the case and retest it. There was silence on the phone. I thought that I had offended him. Then I thought that maybe it had already been done, and he was just laughing. But his answer back was, "Oh my God, do you think that's possible?" I told him that I thought it was possible if we could find it. But I wanted him to be okay with it and wanted him on board and have his support. I wouldn't do it unless his family felt it was the right thing to do. He said, "Yes, do it!"

Q. We should talk about Bob Crane and his relationships. Bob Crane Jr.'s mother is still alive, and Crane's first wife?

A. Yes, Ann Terzian.

Q. He ended up divorcing her after having three kids, and he remarried his second wife, who was on the *Hogan's Heroes* TV show, correct?

A. Yes, Sigrid Valdis. She was the second Fräulein Hilda. The first one was Fräulein Helga. Crane also bedded her, by the way, and her husband, as Bob Crane Jr. told me, basically gave her an ultimatum to "get off the show and get away from Crane or I'm divorcing you" So, she did after one season. She was gone, and Sigrid Valdis came in as Colonel Klink's buxom secretary, the same sort of typecasting. Crane ended up bedding her too and marrying her in this case.

Q. How did Bob Crane meet his friend that would later be accused of murdering him, John Carpenter?

A. I'm writing a blog about their relationship because Crane didn't have many close male friends particularly. Carpenter came onto the scene, introduced to him by Richard Dawson, who played the role of Peter Newkirk on *Hogan's Heroes*.

So, in the mid-sixties, Richard Dawson was friends with this John Carpenter, who was one of the first national video sales reps for

Sony Electronics. Remember, home video at this time was industrial. The general public couldn't get it and didn't even know it existed. But the well-heeled in Hollywood was starting to get their hands on this primarily industrial technology, and the idea that you could tape television shows and save them, the idea that you could tape home movies, keep them, and play them on demand, was fascinating.

Dawson had been doing this with Carpenter. Carpenter had taught him how to use this equipment. Carpenter had taught a lot of famous people how to use this equipment. He claimed to have taught Elvis Presley how to do it. He claimed to have taught the Smothers Brothers, Red Skelton, and others how to use this technology. So, the famous were getting their hands on it. Dawson introduces Carpenter to Crane on the set of *Hogan's Heroes*, and Carpenter and Crane struck up this fast friendship fueled primarily by their love of electronics, Crane's love of photography, and their mutual obsession with women and picking up women.

Q. There were rumors of Richard Dawson and Bob Crane not liking each other. Is that true?

A. It's absolutely true – no question about it. When *Hogan's Heroes* started, the script came to Bob Crane, who was pretty new in the television world. He had guest shots on the *Donna Reed Show* and the *Dick Van Dyke Show*. He was getting some work, but he had never been cast as a lead character, and he was looking for that break. It came in the script of *Hogan's Heroes*, which he thought was brilliant.

But Dawson was much more accomplished on television, and when the script came to him, he thought that he should be Colonel Hogan. But they said, "No, you are a British guy, and that's not going to work." But Dawson really harbored that resentment that he was the second banana. He didn't like that. He felt that he should have been the star. So, there was tension between Crane and Dawson, which was really curious because when John Carpenter came to Scottsdale to visit Bob

Crane the week he was murdered, Carpenter was playing both sides of the fence, trying not to offend Richard Dawson.

So, when he went back to L.A., he told Richard Dawson, "I just happened to be in Phoenix on business and saw that Bob was playing at the Windmill Dinner Theatre, and so I went and paid him a visit." That was a total lie. John Carpenter had planned to meet Bob Crane out on the road in Scottsdale. They made arrangements to fly him in, and Crane picked him up at Sky Harbor Airport when he arrived that Sunday before Crane's murder. So, they were in cahoots together.

Q. What exactly happened on the day of the murder?

A. As would be typical, Carpenter told his employer, at that time in 1978, it was Akai Electronics, that he was going out on the road extensively for a "business trip." But it had nothing to do with business. Carpenter went out on the road and met Crane at various cities Crane was playing dinner theatre.

By this point, *Hogan's* was off the air, and Crane was playing dinner theatres to pay the bills. He was playing in a production of *Beginner's Luck* that he largely directed, produced, and acted in – a four-person play, and it was here in Scottsdale for a one month run.

Carpenter came and visited him in Scottsdale strictly. There was one afternoon of very minor business, but that was it. He visited a video shop up in north Phoenix to cat around every night trying to pick up women and go back to their usual thing.

They were actually having a string of bad luck together. Crane was having sex with women on his own, but he and Carpenter together were not making any headway on the trip to Scottsdale. There's evidence at this point that Crane was becoming tired of Carpenter hanging around. He didn't need Carpenter's video expertise by this time because Crane had become an expert himself in this technology. It had become easier to operate, and Crane knew how to do it. He didn't need this guy hanging around. He even told Bob Crane Jr. before the trip to Scottsdale, "Carpenter's becoming a pain in the ass. He's a hanger-on. I need to make changes." There's evidence that he was going to break off this relationship or at least try and create distance between the two.

Carpenter comes into town, and they "cat around," their usual thing. But on this trip, and this is very interesting, Carpenter usually stayed with Crane in his two-bedroom apartment provided by the theatre. On this particular trip, Carpenter is booked into a hotel down the street from Crane. It looks like he's trying to emancipate a little bit to get some separation from this guy. He doesn't want him hanging around the apartment all the time. It made him uncomfortable.

Then the night of June 28th and going into the early morning hours of June 29, 1978, Crane performs in his dinner theatre, and when they're done with the dinner theatre, they go out to Crane's Monte Carlo car, they had gone there together, and the rear tire was flat in the darkened parking lot of the Windmill Dinner Theatre. Kind of suspicious that on the night he was murdered, he had a flat tire. They determined someone let the air out. The question was if it was a prank by a kid, or was it something more nefarious? Or did somebody try and disable his car so that they could whack him in the parking lot?

Typical Crane, instead of changing it, he didn't want to be bothered with that. He said, "Forget it, let's just drive to the Arco station," which was just 300 yards away. "Let's just drive it there and get it fixed." They got the tire changed, and they drove back to Crane's apartment. He gets into a heated argument with his second wife, who I've already established was Fräulein Hilda on the show. They were in the middle of a divorce. Crane was in a heated argument over the telephone with her. He hung up the phone, slammed it down, and came out saying, "That woman, that woman."

Carpenter was in the front room where all of the camera equipment was, and Crane was fuming. He says, "Let's go find some music. Let's get out of here." So, they went out to Scottsdale and started to weave their magic to pick up some women.

Later that night, they met a woman at a bar named Carole Newell, and Crane was going to meet another woman Carolyn Baare. They all decide to meet at a coffee shop in Carpenter's hotel. It's the Safari Coffee Shop in the Sunburst Hotel. So, they all met there at the Safari. Carpenter had this young girl, Carole Newell, who was about 20, a pretty young girl, who they met in the club that night. Really though, she was attracted to Crane and fascinated that she was hanging out with "Colonel Hogan." Crane doesn't have anybody that he met, so he called Carolyn Baare, who he had been trying to date and trying to bed for the last week or two in Scottsdale. He never did.

But he called her and said they were going to the Safari coffee shop and told her to come to meet them. It's about 1:00 a.m.

now by this time. All four of them sit there and gab about videotaping and the usual stuff Crane was into. Then, they part company. Carpenter walked out in the parking lot. The four of them walked out kind of separated by a little bit of distance, and Carpenter took Newell back to his hotel, the Sunburst. They rolled around on the bed for a little bit, and then she said, "I got to work in the morning, and I got to get up and get out of here." Carpenter was actually a gentleman and said, "Okay." And he drove her home.

Crane, at this time, was striking out with Carolyn Baare in the parking lot. He was trying to get her to come to his apartment. He was asking her if he could come to her apartment. She was a little older and wiser as she was in her forties. She knew his game and what he was up to. She knew that he wanted to have sex with her, and that's all he wanted. She refused his advances, and they parted ways.

After Carpenter dropped off Newell, he went back to his hotel. Crane, in the meantime, had struck out and gone home. According to Carpenter, Crane was up late editing a copy of *Saturday Night Fever* for his 7-year-old son, Scotty, who was the son by the second marriage. He was trying to edit all of the swear words out of *Saturday Night Fever*. That's what Carpenter claimed when he called Crane from his hotel.

During the call, Carpenter asked him, "What are you doing?"

"I struck out. How about you?"

"I struck out too." They were talking, and Crane was supposedly editing *Saturday Night Fever*, so then they hung up the phone.

Carpenter claimed that he then packed up for the morning because he was leaving. He called him again and asked him what he was doing. Again, the same story, Crane was in his boxer shorts editing *Saturday Night Fever*. It was discussed during these two conversations that Crane was going to take Carpenter to the airport that morning. That had been the plan. Crane was going to take Carpenter to Sky Harbor Airport and send him off to L.A. and get back to his business.

Somehow that plan changed. Carpenter ended up driving himself to the airport that morning. The question is why. Was it because they had made different arrangements, or was it because his ride had been murdered? Maybe by his hands.

So, Carpenter took a cab to Sky Harbor, got back to L.A., and Crane's body was discovered about 12 hours later.

Q. It's important to say that in that car, they found blood and brain matter, from what I understand?

A. That's right. They found both if you believe investigators. But one of those was a little bit endowed, and I'll explain. After Carpenter left town, he rented his own car because he wasn't staying with Crane on that particular trip. They had changed the arrangements. Not only did Carpenter have his own hotel room, but he also had his own car.

So, he had rented a 1978 Chrysler Cordova Blue on White. A day after the murder, when the police tracked the car down after becoming a little bit suspicious about this John Carpenter guy when they searched the car, it had bloodstains on the right passenger door. Seven smears, smudges, or streaks of blood. Nothing on the driver's side, though, curiously. Why would it be on the passenger side and not on the driver's side if John Carpenter was driving the car? So, they found blood, but it was not a lot. I don't know if you've seen the pictures of it. When we dove into the evidence, there were all the photographs of it, and it was fascinating. It's not a lot of blood, but there was one pronounced streak at the very top of the door on the Blue vinyl. The State Police did the testing, and it came back Type B blood. Any guess what blood type Bob Crane had?

Q. B.

A. B. Found in only 9 percent of the population. A very rare blood type. So, now you can imagine Carpenter propels to the top of the list of suspects. He's one of the last guys to see him. They're close friends. They've been hanging out. They're living this sorted lifestyle. Videotaping sex and now blood is found in his car. You can imagine what the police are thinking.

So, they fly out to L.A. to interview John Carpenter, and where is he? Carpenter was not at his apartment. He was staying with Richard Dawson in Beverly Hills. But Carpenter doesn't tell police that. He tells police he was at his mother's house 70 miles away, and "it would take me a while to get back, but I'll come back and talk to you."

But he was actually staying that weekend, after he returned from the murder, at Richard Dawson's place. That is such an interesting move, isn't it? Did he think that possibly it could look completely innocent, by the way? Because the people who believe John Carpenter was innocent say, "This is just an innocent guy, and he was hanging out with his buddy for the weekend."

It did provide a little bit of buffer from the police. Here you've got a celebrity, and that makes it a little bit tougher. They have to tread a little more lightly. Investigators thought that he went there as a kind of "cone of safety" from the cops. Make it a little harder for them to find him. And if you found him, you'd have this Richard Dawson-star thing where you'd have to tread very lightly.

Q. Why did he feel that he had to lie to the police about being at his mother's?

A. My guess is that he didn't want to get Dawson involved and wanted to keep Dawson out of it. Maybe Dawson told him, "Don't tell them where you are. I don't want to get involved in this thing." There are theories about whether Carpenter may have talked to Dawson about what happened in Scottsdale, if, in fact, he had killed Crane.

That is in doubt, by the way – whether Carpenter was the killer. Police became very focused on John Carpenter. The issue with the blood is very interesting. And you mentioned the brain splat in the car and the tissue splat in the car. The tissue was not discovered until years later, when they got ready to put Carpenter on trial.

A guy by the name of Jim Raines, who was a former Phoenix Police Investigator, got involved in the case in the nineties. The Maricopa County's office brought him in to reopen this case to take a fresh look at it. When Raines started reexamining this case because Carpenter was never brought to trial or charged, they just didn't feel they had enough evidence. No one was brought in. It was a cold case. They decided to reopen in around 1990.

So, Raines came in and wanted to see the pictures of the Cordova, the evidence photos. They could only find six photos of the car. This was the lynchpin of the case, and they couldn't find the photos. He thought they had to have taken more than six photos. This was ridiculous. He started moving heaven and earth, trying to find those photographs. They finally located them in a DPS storage locker. When they found them, it was a role of 21. An investigator early on had gone through the pictures and determined what he had thought was important and germane, and discarded the rest.

In one of the pictures, not only was there blood on the door, but there was a speck of something else on the door. He figured that it was tissue. But what had happened to that photo? The guy had discarded it because he just didn't think it was important. Raines was looking at it, saying, "This is a smoking gun." He started going to pathologists and getting professional opinions of what was in that photo. The pathologists all agreed that it was adipose tissue – fatty tissue from under the human skull. That's what they believed it was.

Now, if you've got brain tissue in Carpenter's rental car and blood matching the victim's blood type, I think you got your guy. It's great that they had the photograph, but they could never find the vial with the tissue in it. They never collected it, which is what Dennis Borkenhagen, one of the Scottsdale investigators, told me. He thinks they flicked it off the door and didn't realize the significance. Some people think it was collected, put in a vial, but lost during the 16 years between the murder and the time that John Carpenter finally went on trial.

That was the killer with the jury. When Carpenter was finally brought up on charges, largely because of that photograph, that was really a key. "We've got human tissue." That's what they said at first. "We've got human tissue in the car." But that was evidence the former prosecutors didn't have. They only had a picture of it. They didn't have the actual tissue.

With the jury, and I spend a lot of time talking about the Jury Foreman, Michael Lake, who described to me in detail, and it's fascinating what went on in that jury room. There were jurors who said, "This guy did it, but we can't prove it. We don't have it. There's reasonable doubt. The blood type matched Bob Crane, but we don't know for sure that it's not Type B from somebody else. We've got this tissue, but it's a picture. It looks suspicious, but we don't have the actual tissue."

In fact, the judge gave the jury a "Willits Instruction" going into deliberation.

In a "Willits Instruction," a jury is told that if it finds "that the state allowed material evidence to be destroyed," or, in some circumstances, failed to preserve evidence, it may "infer that the evidence would be against the interests of the state." State v.[2]

When the prosecution presents you with something that they don't actually have in their physical possession, you can disregard it. That's where they were. The jury felt if they could have proved that that blood was Bob Crane's, not just type B but his, they would have convicted him.

Because Michael Lake was a former marine, a by-the-book, by-the-rule guy, he was a very important figure in John Carpenter's acquittal because he kept the jury on task. He told them that they couldn't go with their gut feeling. They had to go with the facts. So, they acquitted John Carpenter in 1994, and the case went cold until we dove back into it. We thought maybe we could prove what the prosecution could not 20 years after.

Q. Let's talk about the blood being on the passenger side and the murder weapon, as I hear they are connected.

A. Well, the police believe that as time went on, they weren't sure what killed Bob Crane. They knew he had been struck violently twice in the skull, on the left side of his head with a blunt instrument. It took some time to get to the point where they believed that the murder weapon was a camera tripod from Crane's living room.

Crane had two Quickset Jr. tripods. He used one for the video camera and one to mount the still camera. One of them was missing in his apartment when police went in. It took them years to realize this, though. They didn't realize it at first. Jim Raines started pouring through the porn videos in Crane's apartment. Not only in Scottsdale but in Dallas, which was the stop before. They realized while looking at those tapes that there were two tripods in his possession, and yet only one was found in the apartment when Crane was murdered. So, they figured that he was murdered by a collapsed camera tripod. Not while extended, but while collapsed, where it would be like a baseball bat.

Q. Where is it now?

A. It was never found. Investigators were divided on what happened to it. I believe Carpenter dumped it out in the desert. Possibly at the Indian Reservation down the road. I think that's likely if he was the killer, or that the killer did that. Or maybe a dumpster. The dumpsters in the immediate area were searched, though. Jim Raines believes that if Carpenter were the killer, he might have packed it in his suitcase. This was before TSA. It would have fit in his suitcase, and he could have flown back to L.A. with it.

But the theory is that Carpenter propped up the tripod in the front passenger seat and leaned it against the passenger door. Still with some blood on it, even though it may have been wrapped up in a towel. As the car moved and his brakes were applied, the tripod would have slid along that upper part of the passenger door, and that was what deposited the blood. That was their theory.

Q. What was the process for you to get that blood retested?

A. It was so unbelievable that they allowed me to do it. It took months to find the original evidence. It was in 11 boxes in the County Attorney's office in their evidence room. It's possible they may have stalled me. They were going to cooperate but do it at their own pace, thinking I might just get fed up and move on. But to their credit, the County Attorney said, "If John wants to do this, I have no problem with it if it will bear fruit. If it's worth his time and ours."

They had to find the evidence. They found the evidence boxes, and for months after that, they couldn't find the blood evidence. They were going through the boxes, one by one, but remember they had fresh cases coming in, so devoting manpower to this was a problem. They had to go through those boxes and recategorize everything that was in them. Because after the trial, they dumped everything into 11 boxes. The boxes were all jumbled and mismarked. They didn't put the stuff back in the original boxes, so it made it very confusing.

The samples from the car were what we sent off to Bode Cellmark Forensics, which is the same lab in Virginia that did the evidence for OJ and Jon Benet Ramsey's case. Everything they did on Crane's case back then came back inconclusive in Carpenter's rental car. My theory was that this time we were going to get a hit, and we did. It just wasn't what anybody expected. It was a bombshell. Bode told me because I was a client, "We don't have a protocol for this. We have never done this for a reporter before. We're usually dealing with law enforcement and defense attorneys." We paid for the testing. Fox 10 and I did.

Q. It didn't turn out to be Bob Crane's blood, did it?

A. It turned out that it was not Bob Crane's blood in John Carpenter's car. The sample came back, and we were expecting that it was going to be Bob Crane's blood. No questions in our minds. But that's not what we got.

We got a DNA profile, two of them – one partial that was too degraded to make any conclusions, and the major contributor, which is known to be a man of unknown origin. We don't know who that person is or why that DNA was in that car. That was a bombshell.

I tell you without a doubt that if they had this resolved in 1994, I do not believe they would have put John Carpenter on trial. That's how big this is. The defense would have just said, "Look, you tested the stuff, and it's not even Bob Crane's blood. What are you doing here? Why do you keep haranguing this John Carpenter?"

Even though everything points to Carpenter, there is doubt.

Q. In the video *Murder in Scottsdale* by Robert Graysmith, there were claims the police didn't do a good job or take care of the crime scene. They let people come and go, people smoked, and they used Crane's telephone. In fact, they brought Victoria Berry back into the apartment and let her answer the telephone, and she even smoked in the apartment. What do you think Victoria Berry has to do with this case?

Victoria Berry had been touring for months with Bob Crane in *Beginner's Luck* when the play landed in Scottsdale in June 1978. The Australian born actress, then 28, had been seeking stardom for years, to no avail. As always, Hollywood had more than enough busty blondes, and Berry's efforts largely failed, despite some close brushes with success. She auditioned for a plum role on *Charlie's Angels* after Farrah Fawcett-Majors quit, but Cheryl Ladd won out. She was set to play Marilyn Monroe in a movie to be called *Saint Marilyn,* but the deal fell through. Her biggest break in show business probably came when she was cast as the go-go dancer in the credits of *Starsky and Hutch*. In the late 1970s, Berry hit the dinner-theatre circuit to pay the bills and to work on her acting skills. The gig with Crane was easy enough, and unlike some of his other colleagues, she got along fine with him.[3]

A. I don't think Victoria Berry had anything to do with it. She just happened to come to the apartment that afternoon on a mission that she and Crane had set up the day before. She was there to overdub a scene from *Beginner's Luck,* the play that they were doing. They were to overdub her voice because there had been some audio problems. In fact, John Carpenter had taped that scene at the Windmill the week that Crane was murdered. That footage still exists.

I don't believe Victoria Berry had anything to do with it. I don't believe her husband Alan Wells had anything to do with it. People have talked about him.

I think the possibilities come down to: is there somebody the police simply do not know about, someone that they completely missed, that it might not have been one of his acquaintances, or somebody unknown to the police that may have entered his apartment and killed him.

Q. In your book, you talk about DNA possibly being a problem?

A. The problem with the DNA is, and I don't know if you have talked to other authors of true crime who have discussed this, but it is an area that I'm starting to explore. DNA has become so sensitive, and they can bore in so tight now that the tests can sometimes pick up what I call in the book "Outlier DNA."

Touch DNA, also known as Trace DNA, is a forensic method for analyzing DNA left at the scene of a crime. It is called "touch DNA" because it only requires very small samples, for example, from the skin cells left on an object after it has been touched or casually handled or from footprints.[4]

> In other words, if you magnify it so much, you may not only get the car door from John Carpenter's car and DNA from the blood that might have been there at one time, you might pick up DNA from the Investigator who was swabbing it. You might get DNA from the guy who was at the factory and assembled the car door. This is the problem now with DNA. It's actually complicating things in certain cases because you can pick up things that have nothing to do with the crime that sends police and investigators down dark alleys going nowhere.
>
> You're getting DNA, but what does it mean? Juries are demanding this now. They almost want science to make their decision

for them. DNA is not the "be-all and end-all" of everything. It can mislead investigators at times. But there is a reliance and an expectation now. The "CSI effect" that you are going to have and produce it for the jury and the crime is going to be solved in 30 minutes in an episode of CSI, and it's just not that simple.

Q. What do you think the unknown DNA tells us?

A. Think about this for a minute. If it's Carpenter, and you just murdered a man, you have some low-velocity blood spatter on your person as well. You can clean it up in Crane's apartment, to a certain degree. Maybe even put on one of Crane's shirts or jackets so that you are hiding the blood. You wash your hands and all of that, but you still got the murder weapon that you've got to put in the passenger side of the car. There's blood on the passenger side, but nothing on the driver's side.

Now we're assuming Carpenter did this alone. He's the killer in the driver's side of the car, and they find nothing on the driver's side. Doesn't that strike you as odd? If he deposits the murder weapon, gets rid of it, takes it out of the passenger side door, and deposits it somewhere out in the desert or the dumpster, he's going to get blood on him again when he gets back in the car. Why no blood on the steering wheel? Why no blood on the console or the driver's side door handle? Nothing. Nothing.

Q. Was someone else involved in the crime? Maybe even driving?

A. Well, this is the question. This does raise that possibility, I think. People have theorized about this as well. This is what John Carpenter's attorney, Stephen Avilla, believed. He believed that there were two people involved, and one was a woman. He believed a woman had sex with Bob Crane and killed him. He said it live on our program when we unveiled this on television last November. Avilla was thrilled that we had done this because he said, "Finally, his client, John Carpenter, has been vindicated. This proves he was not the killer."

Investigators wanted to say the DNA tests we got back have problems because you could be getting "phantom DNA." Let me explain that for just one moment. By the time we tested the samples of vinyl from John Carpenter's car, we had two samples cut out of vinyl in snap-cap tubes. Those had already been tested four times back in the 60s and 90s before we got a hold of them.

One of the samples literally had nothing on it. Nothing was detectable. It had been washed clean. Remember back in the 70s when they were just swabbing for blood, they would swab the whole stain and get a blood sample because they weren't looking for DNA. They didn't know about DNA then. The other sample was a piece of felt from the middle of the car door on the passenger side. Decorative felt that was much more porous had DNA on it. But no visible blood. By the time we tested it, there was no visible blood left on these samples. So, all we're left with is DNA from what was once a sample that had blood on it but not visible anymore.

If it were blood on that sample and we tested it, it would have had the highest concentration of DNA that you could have. Why did we get nothing from Bob Crane? Wouldn't you expect something if that were Bob Crane's blood?

Q. Was there signs of recent sexual activity with Bob Crane?

A. He had semen on his right thigh, dried semen on his right thigh and lower right abdomen. That was present at his autopsy. The Scottsdale detective who was present at the autopsy urged the Medical Examiner to scrape it and save it. The Medical Examiner gruffly told him, "What's that going to tell you? He had a piece of ass before he died." They wanted to collect it because there was a theory that the killer might have masturbated over Bob Crane's body as a final "F.U." to the victim.

A lot has been said about the police work being sloppy at the scene. It was not a perfect investigation. I will say letting people into the apartment like Victoria Berry to make her statement was not perfect. It was 104 or 105 degrees outside. So, they were trying to find a place to get her in and make her statement. They should have taken her down to the police department, but they didn't.

The Medical Examiner cut the chord from Crane's head, which was not totally inconsistent, but shaving Crane's head, in his bed, at the crime scene. He shaved his head with a straight razor around the wounds to get a better look at the wounds. That did contaminate the crime scene. With all that said, investigators still argued, "This has been overblown. That even though it was imperfect, and things happened that were not right, they basically got to the right conclusion."

Q. What's your thought about the second wife and Bob Crane's will removing the first wife and kids from the will? They were also in the middle of a bad divorce at the time.

A. Yes, a bitter divorce. This was Bob Crane Jr.'s theory all along. Carpenter comes number one, and Crane's wife comes number two because she had money to gain. They were in the middle of a divorce. What more convenient way for her to score financially than for him to be rubbed out right in the middle of their divorce. She would get everything. That was Bob Crane Jr.'s theory.

Police records, phone records, flight records, all of that shows that she was in Bainbridge Island, Washington, when the murder happened. Remember, she and Crane had had a phone conversation that night. The phone records back that up. They had spoken that night, and she was in Washington on vacation with her son, Scotty. So, she would not have had the opportunity to kill Bob Crane because she was too far away, and she could never have caught a flight down here. There weren't any.

Q. Did she put somebody up to it?

A. She could have put Carpenter up to it. But she did not like John Carpenter at all because he was the source of all evil in her mind for her husband. You know, catting around and causing Bob to do all of this crazy stuff, or at least aiding and abetting. The idea that she would have suddenly befriended him and got him to do this just doesn't make sense. Did she hire someone else? There's just no evidence of it.

Q. Crane was going to become very wealthy in a matter of a few years after his death, wasn't he?

A. You know, I think they felt there was some money to be made, but I don't think anyone in their wildest dreams thought that *Hogan's Heroes* in reruns was going to be so wildly popular. That show got airplay for years. The guy who cashed in was Sumner Redstone with Viacom. That's who really cashed in. I think they made $90 million off that in the end through reruns.

It's bittersweet for me to watch them because I still have the image of Bob Crane's head all bashed in. But he was a really good father by all accounts, and his kids really did love him. He was like a lot of people. There was the side you see publicly, and then there's the dark side.

Q. I'm not sure that I see it as a dark side. I think that's what he needed to exist and to be Bob Crane.

A. Right. Some people say he was ahead of his time. This was the celebrity sex video before Paris Hilton, before Pam Anderson, or before Kim Kardashian.

The difference being that Crane never intended them to become public. Some say he would have been mortified that they were becoming public because he knew it would be career-suicide if they ever got out. He wanted to be Jack Lemon. That was his idol. He wanted to be the next Jack Lemon. He was kind of on that track when *Hogan's Heroes* was running. But this addiction to pornography and sex and all of the stuff he was doing personally really kind of undercut what he was doing professionally. Disney, among others, caught wind of it, and it was hurting his career.

Q. His son Scotty made it public as well, didn't he?

A. He did a pay-per-view site where you could watch Bob Crane's porn. You know, I've seen a lot of it because it was in evidence. It pretty much depicts the same thing. He compliments these women. They take their clothes off, starting with their bra then panties. He is working it, complimenting them, telling them how beautiful they are, and it's very light.

These women, by the way, all knew they were being taped. The equipment back then looked like it fell off the space capsule. It's big, bulky, and you couldn't miss it. He had it all lined up in the living room with the TV facing the couch. You could not miss that this stuff was on, and the women I saw were mugging for the camera. They were enjoying it. They were smiling and having a great time. So, the idea that he was surreptitiously taping these women was nonsense. That did not happen. The only exception would be if they were too drunk to give actual consent, and that was possible.

Q. Now, in the movie *Auto Focus*, they brought up the aspect of John Carpenter possibly being homosexual or bisexual. Did you come across anything about that?

A. Yes. Bob Crane Jr. told police back in 1978 that his dad had told him Carpenter swung both ways and that Carpenter had had a sexual encounter with Richard Dawson. That was one of the more salacious things that we found out. Those two had apparently had a little something going on, according to Bob Crane. Take that with a grain of salt because Bob Crane didn't like Dawson. So, did he put that out there to kind of poison Dawson's reputation? Possibly, or possibly it's true.

Listen to the full interview with John Hook on my website:

houseofmysteryradio/episodes/john-hook-bob-crane

---

1. John Hook - FOX 10 Phoenix. https://www.fox10phoenix.com/person/h/john-hook
2. Arizona Supreme Court. https://www.azcourts.gov/LinkClick.aspx?fileticket=OyvAc19fl_M%3D&portalid=45
3. https://www.phoenixnewtimes.com/news/the-bob-crane-murder-case-part-two-6425966
4. https://en.wikipedia.org/wiki/Touch_DNA

Like father, like son
INTERVIEW WITH ROBERT DAVID CRANE

After doing the interview with John Hook, the natural follow up would be with Bob Crane's son, Bob Crane Jr., who Hook worked with for his own book, and of course, knew all the people who were involved in his father's life.

Robert David Crane is an American author and writer, probably best known for the book *Crane: Sex, Celebrity, and My Father's Unsolved Murder*, about the unsolved murder of his father, *Hogan's Heroes* star, Bob Crane. He was the son of Robert Crane and Anne Terzian, Bob's high school sweetheart, and one of three children they had, including Deborah Anne Crane and Karen Leslie Crane.

A writer for *Playboy Magazine* for over twenty years, he published his first book, *Jack Nicholson, Face to Face*, in 1975, and worked as a publicist for comedian John Candy. They also worked together on the movies *Hamburger*, *Only The Lonely*, *Hostage for a Day*, and *Wagons' East*. Candy also gave Robert a walk-on role in the film, *Delirious*.

In 2002, he collaborated with Director Paul Schrader in the film *Auto Focus*, a semi-autobiographical chronicle on the sordid off-camera life and murder of his father. The film was the subject of controversy with his half-brother Scott Crane and stepmother Sigrid Valdis, who considered it unfair and exploitative and an insult to the memory of Bob Crane.

His other projects include actor Bruce Dern's memoir, *Things I've Said, But Probably Shouldn't Have: An Unrepentant Memoir*, *Jack Nicholson: The Early Years*, and a biography about the life of Tom Mankiewicz, *My Life as a Mankiewicz: An Insider's Journey Through Hollywood*.

Crane also co-produced the short films *Mirage* with Richard Decker, and *She'll Never Make it to the Olympics* with Kari Hildebrand. His most recent book is *Crane: Sex, Celebrity, and My Father's Unsolved Murder*, published in 2015.¹

This interview took place in June of 2018.

Q. Your father's most popular series was *Hogan's Heroes*, but my personal favorite thing that he did was his radio shows.

A. You know, one of the things I'm really proud of about *Hogan's Heroes* was that I was a fan of the show. I was a teenager and used to play army with my buddies and all that kind of stuff, and we used to watch *Combat* with Vic Morrow. But one of the things about Hogan's that I'm really proud about now is that in 1965 when it started, there were exactly two series on television that featured people of color on a regular basis. That's unbelievable. Hogan's was Ivan Dixon, and can you guys name the other show? *I Spy* with Bill Cosby. Those were the only two regular series with people of color in the case.

Q. When your father was recording *Hogan's Heroes*, he was probably at his peak in Hollywood. How close were you with him at that time?

A. I have two younger sisters, and he allowed all of us to be as involved as we wanted to be. But because we were all going to public schools, I would work around that. So, during summer vacation, I would spend on Hogan's and just hang out there. You mentioned his radio show earlier. If he had a guest on one of his shows and I could somehow work that out, a school holiday or something, I would go with him to the radio show and watch him interview the guest. That's kind of how I fit in there.

Q. Did you know about his hidden or alternative lifestyle?

A. Later on in my teenage years. He had a darkroom at home, which I guess most people don't even know what a dark room is anymore. He could develop his own film because it was pre-digital, and he actually used film for his cameras. He would develop the film, and many of the photos were legitimate. You know landscapes, or if my mom and dad went on vacation somewhere, they would take photos. But then I saw a few photos of some women I did not recognize, and that was a little lightbulb going on for me. Unbeknownst to me, my mom and dad were already in discussions about his extracurricular activities. But again, I was 15 or 16 then, and my sisters were much younger. So, they had no idea of this other life.

Q. How did you make sense of all of that within your own family, Bob?

A. We had what I thought was such a normal family. We didn't live in Beverly Hills. My folks didn't drive a Mercedes and have all the glamorous things of that day. We lived in, as the *TV Guide* called it, "unfashionable" Tarzana, California. It was just suburbia. We did get to have a swimming pool. We had friends over and had BBQs. We just thought we were normal. So, it started to shake my foundation when I saw these women. What is this? Because my parents were the rocks of my life. I mean, they were together, and nothing was ever going to change. So, the foundation started to shake at that time.

Q. How did that impact your relationship with your father?

A. Well, my father, left eventually. About a year or two later. I was still a senior in high school. I kind of became the male of the household, which was strange for me because it was always Dad. But he was gone, and I had my mom, two sisters, and grandmother as well. So, I was surrounded by women now. And that was different for me. I was 17, and it was a new footing for me because I've always been taken care of by my mom and dad.

Q. When you saw these photos, did you ever ask about them?

A. No. I didn't say anything to my mom. I didn't have the "cojones" to approach my dad. I just didn't have the nerve. Let me make it clear, too; I wasn't in the darkroom snooping around looking for anything. I was just looking at some of the legit photos that he had taken. I think of his trip to Hawaii or something. I was just looking at them, and I found these.

Q. Did you ever talk to him about this?

A. I sucked it in for years until I could start talking to him a bit in my early twenties. When I got a little more nerve, but it was never like 100 percent like right now as an old man that I am now. As you get older, for me anyhow, I don't mind confronting people about stuff now.

Q. Did what you discovered about him ever shade your opinion of him?

A. It did shade it a little bit. Now I'm starting to find out that there's stuff I don't know about one of my parents. I looked at my parents like they were rulers of the world. They knew everything. They did everything. Later I found out, "no, they didn't." They were faking it just like everything else.

Q. Fast forward a few years after *Hogan's Heroes* ended. Your father then started doing a dinner theatre and rented a room in Scottsdale, Arizona. Were you living with him at that time?

A. Actually, he had started doing plays years earlier, even during Hogan's. So, when Hogan's was off for three months, he would hit the road. Go to Chicago or New Jersey or wherever and do a play. Dinner theatre, at the time, was a big deal. All sorts of people on the way up, or people on the way down, veteran performers, new performers, people with series, they squeezed in the engagements during time off.

When he was doing the engagement in Scottsdale, he didn't get an apartment there. They put him in an apartment just for the run of the show. In other words, he was supposed to play a month in Scottsdale, so they put him up at an apartment instead of a hotel. So, that's the apartment you are referring to. But there's another apartment in L.A., which I was sharing with him at the time of his death. He was going through a divorce from his second wife.

Q. That was Patricia Olson?

A. Yes. She played Colonel Klink's second secretary. She came in Season Two.

Patricia Annette Olson, known by her stage name, "Sigrid Valdis," was an American actress. She was best known for playing "Hilda" in the American television series *Hogan's Heroes*. Valdis' second marriage was to *Hogan's Heroes* star, Bob Crane, on the set of the series on October 16, 1970. Co-star Richard Dawson served as Crane's best man. Following the birth of their son in 1971, Valdis retired from acting. In 1978, she moved from the Los Angeles area after Crane was murdered.[2]

Q. At the time of his murder, Bob was in the middle of a divorce from his second wife, Patricia, correct?

A. Yes.

Q. At the time, you aimed your suspicions towards her. Do you still feel that way?

A. Well, there were always two people in my book. Number one has to be John Carpenter. Not the film director, but the Sony home video salesperson, which is how my dad met him. He would have to rank as number one because he had the means and opportunity. The bottom line for him killing his so-called "friend" was that he lost his friend, which I never understood.

Secondly, though, the person with any financial gain from his death was Patty. She's always been number two on my list. They were legally married at the time of his death and going through a divorce with attorneys and all of that stuff, and she gained the estate. When I say estate, it was no big multimillion estate or anything, but for 1978, it was very comfortable – some cash and a couple of properties. She did fine by it, and she's the one who gained something. It's just weird timing.

Q. How would she have done this?

A. Well, for a while, she claimed to be in Seattle of all places with their son Scotty, who was six or seven at the time. She loved Bainbridge Island, and that's where she claimed to be at the time of the murder. I pushed the Scottsdale police on it and the DA's office in Arizona to really see if you could hop on a plane in Seattle and get to Phoenix during that time span.

Just to back up a sec, at the murder scene, there was no break-in. Nothing was taken except for a booklet of polaroid photos that my dad had taken. Otherwise, it was obviously someone he knew who was there because he went to bed. It was a two-bedroom, and he went to bed. He had to have been comfortable with the person there because, again, no break-in, no forced entry, or anything like that. So, that would mean Carpenter. That would mean Patty. Or maybe someone else that I'm not thinking of.

Q. Yes, because you wouldn't just up and go to bed when there was someone in your house.

A. No. I wouldn't.

Q. Did someone else have a key to the apartment?

A. That's the other possibility. A very strange thing happened ten days before his murder. It was Father's Day. Now, Patty and my dad were going through a really ugly proceeding. It was not pretty. A knock came on the door at his apartment on Father's Day 1978. He opened the door, and it was Patty and Scotty, the young son.

Well, Dad called me the next day and said, "You'll never guess who was here yesterday?" I was wracking my brain and then gave up. I didn't know. Then he said, "Patty." I responded loudly, "Patty?!" He continued, "Yeah. She just showed up at the door with Scotty."

They spent a few hours together, and it was very uncomfortable. But now, it was like she had done a recon mission. She knew where he was. She knew the lay of the land, and then ten days later, he was dead. Strange. Very strange.

Q. He was bludgeoned to death with a tripod, correct?

A. Yes. Now Patty was pretty strong physically. I don't put it past her to do that. But that would have to veer back to Carpenter. He was a video salesperson. That was a big thing at the time, home video. Now people don't know what video is. Home video, that was your own little deck in your camera. And it was instantaneous. You could watch yourself on the monitor. It was very exciting.

So, Carpenter would obviously know about equipment, and he would think of, if it were him, he would think of a murder weapon. The head of a tripod is a very hard metal that can do some major damage, which it did.

There were two blows to the side of my dad's head while he was asleep. Again, that kind of steers back into Carpenter's arena.

Q. Why don't you think that somebody would just take out a hitman or hire someone to kill your dad?

A. A hit, and maybe I've read too many too many Harlan Coben books or something, but if it were a hit, it would have been a gun. In my way of thinking, that would have been clean. It's the term, hitman.

If you had said it was a jealous boyfriend of a girl that he had been seeing in Scottsdale, I would say, okay. But a hit to me is clean. A gun would have been used. It would have been in out, fast. This was a messy two blows to his head. I went to the murder scene after his body was removed. There was spatter all over the walls. It was a mess.

To me, that says more emotion, that kind of a strike. That emotion again would get back to Carpenter, who my dad told the night before, according to witnesses, they were not going to do this anymore. Carpenter used to visit him in different cities around the country when he did the plays, and he became a hanger-on after a while. It was no longer fun for my dad. My dad told me, "Carpenter's becoming a pain in the ass."

Seeing the writing on the wall was like an emotional break-up for Carpenter. For Patty, it was an emotional break-up because they were getting a divorce. So, to me, it would be messier. If it were a mobster hit, or maybe even the boyfriend of a woman who had a gun, you go in there with a gun and boom, boom, you're done, and you walk away.

Q. What was the police's take on all of this?

A. First of all, it happened in the wrong town, unfortunately. Scottsdale is a wonderful place. Beautiful. At the time in

1978, they averaged two murders a year. So, this was like Andy Griffiths and Barney Fife. They had no idea. They were way in over their head. A lot of things have changed in law enforcement. I get it. I understand that.

At the time, people were going into the crime scene, and they were contaminating it. People were touching things. I went there with my dad's attorney the night of the murder. It happened 12 or 15 hours earlier, and we came in and were walking around the crime scene, and I was touching things. People were smoking.

I didn't think about it at the time, but now all these years later, of course, it was pre-DNA, so there was no DNA testing. They were way in over their head. So, they immediately went for Carpenter, the Scottsdale Police Department, because he was in town when it happened. They didn't so much go for Patty. As far as I'm concerned, they never really pursued it. Then, there was talk about a jealous boyfriend, and there was the question, "Did your dad owe money to Chicago mobsters?" Not as far as I knew. It was a little bit cliché. That would have been a professional hit, not a sloppy strike-somebody-in-the-head.

Q. Let's talk about the friendship that he had with Carpenter. The movie about this case suggests that Carpenter was perhaps gay, and he had a relationship with your father that was not just business. That could make more sense if they were ending their partnership or relationship. What are your feelings on that?

A. Again, from conversations with my dad and from hearing things and reading things like you, what I heard was that John Carpenter was bisexual, and he did have relationships with women. He loved young women. He loved teenage women. In fact, there was a charge against Carpenter around that time for being with an underage woman back here in L.A.

I think he was in love with my dad, though. I think he liked hanging out with these so-called TV stars or celebrities. He was always drawn to celebrities because that's who he sold the video products to. He was in love with that. He might have been in love with my dad. From my dad's point of view, again as his son just hearing from my dad, I never got a sense that the love like that was returned. I think it was more of a one-sided thing like they did portray in the movie.

Q. But Crane would still be aware of Carpenter's affection towards him, right?

A. Yes.

Q. Because they were friends with each other for years, correct?

A. Yes.

Q. They had sex with a lot of people together, and they filmed each other having sex. I'm wondering if this could be the passion behind the bludgeoning.

A. Now, there was a weird occurrence the day that the whole story broke. Again, this was June of 1978. This was pre-tweeting, pre-facebooking, pre-instagramming, before cell phones, any of that. So, it didn't get out to the news for a long time.

I was at home at the apartment I was sharing with my dad in Los Angeles. About 3 o'clock in the afternoon, I receive a phone call from John Carpenter on his return to L.A. The thing that was weird about that was that he never had any reason to call me. He said, "Hey Bobby, how are you? I'm back in L.A. and if you need anything, let me know." I said, "Oh, okay. How did it go?" That was it. Thirty seconds and hung up with him. After that, I was looking at the phone, wondering what that was all about.

Sometimes, he would call me on his way out and say something like, "Bobby, I need to pick up the patch cord that goes from the camera to the deck. Your dad needs this, and I'm going to be seeing him in Columbus, Ohio on Thursday." So, he would come by and get that. But it was never on the way back.

After I got off the phone with Carpenter and I got a weird feeling, I figured I'd call my dad. It was 3:00 or 3:20 that afternoon. My dad had now been dead, they think about 12 hours. I called his apartment in Scottsdale, and a woman answered. It was Victoria Berry, who was in the play. There were only four people in the play. She played the sexy, young woman that he's having an affair with in the play. She answered the phone, and I asked if my dad was around, and she told me that he was out right now. So, I told her to let him know that Bobby called, and she said she would. Turns out, later I found out that she was surrounded by Scottsdale police and detectives. They were having her pick up the phone like nothing was wrong.

They think he was killed around 3:00 or 3:30 in the morning, and this was around 3:30 in the afternoon. Then, I found out that Carpenter made other phone calls. He called the dinner theatre in the afternoon looking for my dad. Well, wait a minute. The show didn't go on until 8 o'clock, so my dad would get to the theatre, knowing my dad, 7:50. Carpenter also called a couple of other people in Scottsdale. Kind of like covering his tracks. I found out all of this later.

Q. How is your relationship with Patty and your half-brother Scotty now? I know that after your father's death, Scotty created a pay-for website with your father's pornography films that he took of himself with others.

A. That website was, I think, in the late nineties, 98, 99, or 2000. Somebody told me about it, and it was Patty and Scotty that had dug out all of these old photos. They found all of the videos and photos that he made in his apartment. Instead of just putting them away or burning them, they decided that they were going to make some money off it. So, this was the loving wife that she claims to be or claimed to be since she's no longer with us. A loving wife that would put your husband's private photos out there on the internet and charge money! That really broke open all of his secrets to the world. They were nobody's business. He took photos for himself or the person he was taking the photo of. They would ask for photos, but it wasn't for the world wide web to see.

So, to answer your question, I have no relationship with Scotty. I did have a relationship with Patty early on in my dad and Patty's relationship. Again, trying to all become this happy family. That worked for a couple of years until Patty basically had no room for any other women in her life. That would include my sisters, my Mom, of course, being the ex-wife, my dad's mother, my grandmother, who was still alive at that time. So, the women kind of went first. I survived for a while. We got along, but then in one of their arguments, I, of course, took my dad's side.

Q. Did Patty know that your dad was making all of these videos of sex with Carpenter?

A. Yes, she did. She endorsed it early on. She told him to go ahead, and when he was

LIKE FATHER, LIKE SON

on the road, to go ahead and have some fun. That fell apart after a while.

Listen to the full interview with Robert Crane Jr. on my website:

houseofmysteryradio/episodes/bob-crane-robert-crane-jr

---

1. Robert David Crane | The Delirious Movie Wikia | Fandom. https://ashfordfalls.fandom.com/wiki/Robert_David_Crane
2. https://en.wikipedia.org/wiki/Sigrid_Valdis

PART IV
Natalie Wood

Natalie Wood, born Natalia Nikolaevna Zakharenko, was an American actress who began her career in film as a child actor at age four. At age eight, she co-starred in *Miracle on 34th Street*. She successfully transitioned to young adult roles. She was the recipient of four Golden Globes and received three Academy Award nominations: Best Supporting Actress in Rebel Without A Cause, and Best Actress for *Splendor in the Grass*, and *Love with the Proper Stranger*.

Sadly, Wood drowned off Catalina Island on November 29, 1981, at age 43, during a holiday break from the production of *Brainstorm* with her co-star Christopher Walken and husband, Robert Wagner.

The events surrounding her death have been the subject of conflicting witness statements, prompting the Los Angeles County Sheriff's Department, under the instruction of the coroner's office, to list her cause of death as "drowning and other undetermined factors" in 2012.

In 2018, Robert Wagner was named as a person of interest in the ongoing investigation into her death.[1]

1. htttps://en.wikipedia.org/wiki/Natalie_Wood

The Ship's Captain
INTERVIEW WITH MARTI RULLI

Marti Rulli was born and raised in New Jersey. While working in both newspapers and magazines for over 25 years, Marti was a freelance writer for various publications. When called upon by her longtime friend, Dennis Davern, the former Captain of the yacht, "Splendour," owned by celebrities, to tell Davern's firsthand account of the night legendary actress Natalie Wood died, Marti took on the project as a journalist and as an investigator. *Goodbye Natalie, Goodbye Splendour* is Marti Rulli's first book.

Marti used her investigation to appeal to the Los Angeles County Sheriff Department to reopen the

Wood case in November 2011. As a result of the pending investigation, Natalie Wood's death is no longer officially classified as accidental.

This interview was in 2016.

Q. What was your connection to Natalie Wood?

A. My friend Dennis Davern, who I met when I was a teenager and after he got out of the Navy, worked at a marina in Florida. He took his sport fisherman boat to California to sell. Dennis was one of the crew members that took the boat to California.

At that time, Robert Wagner and Natalie Wood were yacht shopping. They happen to really like this boat that Davern had brought to California and ended up purchasing it. They also hired Dennis as their captain. Dennis was like a family friend and had been friends for years, so one of my best friends starting working for one of my favorite actresses.

He would start telling me things about the couple, just some personal things about them, like their favorite ice cream and what they liked to do on weekends. It was just really nice having my friend work for famous people.

Q. So, what can you tell us about the couple?

A. Robert Wagner and Natalie Wood were married twice, and they were *the* couple of Hollywood. They were the Brad Pitt and Angelina Jolie of their time. But they had a troubled marriage. They were divorced and then remarried. Their second marriage was a very happy marriage, but Robert Wagner was jealous of Natalie. And not only of her co-stars but of her status in the business. Natalie was a mega superstar from a child actress onto an adult actress.

Robert Wagner had worked in some movies and became very popular in TV with *Switch, It Takes a Thief,* and then his most famous *Hart to Hart,* but he had never established what Natalie had established in the movie industry.

So, I just had this information about Natalie and Robert Wagner through my friend who worked for them. He was their captain for about seven years and ended up in the middle of one of the largest mysteries in Hollywood history – Natalie Wood's death.

Dennis saw much, much more than he had ever told in the beginning. That's because he was told to never talk about what really happened. But it worked on his conscience, and he called me his friend. I worked for a newspaper, but he trusted that I would not do anything with the information. He told me what really happened to Natalie in the 1980s.

Q. What did you do about what Dennis told you?

A. I wanted the Los Angeles County Sheriff's office to get involved back then, but it was a closed case, and they would not listen to me. They were just content to keep the case closed. It took me 30 years of effort. And believe me, I put effort into it.

I started recording everything. I started writing a book, which I promised the original detectives on the case that I would not publish if they take another look at Natalie's death. They refused. So, in 2009, I allowed my book to be published. It tells the truth about what happened to Natalie on her final weekend. That wasn't enough either.

So, then I gathered testimonial statements from people that I had interviewed and researched, forensic testing that I had done myself, and I presented this package to the Los Angeles County Sheriff's Department, along with a petition an attorney had started to get the Wood case reopened. Two weeks after they received that package in 2011, they contacted us. They came to interview us, and the new Natalie Wood investigation began.

Q. So, the police have reopened the case?

A. Yes. In November 2011, the case was reopened, and they had 30 years of information to go through. But they announced it and put it out there that if anyone has any additional information, please bring it forward, which a lot of people did. There were other people near the boat who saw exactly what Dennis Davern saw happen the night of Natalie Wood's death. So, new witnesses that corroborated Dennis's story had come forward.

They also reviewed Natalie Wood's autopsy results. The first time I saw the diagram of all the bruises on her body, I knew I was looking at a battered woman. I cannot for the life of me understand how it was overlooked in 1981 when Natalie died on Thanksgiving weekend. But it was; the case was closed. They now have medical evidence, scientific evidence, new witnesses, and just last year, they named Robert Wagner a "person of interest" in his wife's death.

Q. Have the detectives brought Robert Wagner in for any type of questioning?

A. Robert Wagner refuses to cooperate with the new investigation. And he hired a criminal attorney who claims that Wagner has cooperated fully. He has not. In 1981, he answered a few questions right before the case was closed, which was within days. He put out a statement when the case was reopened in 2011 that he welcomed the new investigation into his wife's death, and anything he or his family could do to help, he would do – as long as it's not based on those wanting to profit from the 30th anniversary of Natalie's death.

It was a little jab at Dennis and me for having accomplished what we accomplished. But he has not cooperated with the new detectives on the case. He will not answer any questions for them. When Sheriff Barker was the Sheriff a few years back, they even went to Wagner's house in Aspen, Colorado, and Robert Wagner would not let them in. Not only that, Natalie's two daughters have refused to even listen to the detectives. But Natalie's younger sister, Lana Wood, who was also an actress, a "Bond girl," cared about what happened to her sister.

So, they disowned her from the family. But at least the detectives have a blood relative who wants justice for her sister. The new detectives on the case stay in touch with Lana. They let her know what's happening. After they reviewed the old autopsy report of Natalie's, they saw the mistakes made. For instance, Natalie had over 300 ccs of urine in her bladder, which indicates that medically Natalie was not conscious in the water. Therefore, leading to the question, how did her body get into the water?

Then, they have Dennis Davern's account, plus two other witnesses who pretty much saw how Natalie might have gotten into the water because there was a huge argument on the rear of the boat moments before Natalie went missing from the boat.

Q. Dennis Davern, why did he not tell the truth back at the time of Natalie's death?

THE SHIP'S CAPTAIN 249

A. He regretted it immediately. But what happened was that after Natalie was missing, Robert Wagner started to pour a Scotch for Dennis, and Dennis became very nervous. He knew something terrible had happened. He wasn't quite sure what. They had all been drinking out to dinner. Christopher Walken was the only other guest on board. He was Natalie's co-star in *Brainstorm*, and Christopher was already in his cabin asleep when everything went down.

Dennis was told by Robert Wagner, "Here's what we're going to say. We don't know what happened to Natalie. She took the dingy, and we are waiting for her to return." It took hours before they called for help, and Dennis had pleaded with Robert Wagner to turn on the searchlight, which could see for a half a mile in the area. Robert Wagner refused. This is his wife missing at sea, but he refused to turn on a spotlight.

Dennis asked him to call for help. He refused to call for help. Dennis was very young at the time. He was in his twenties, but a young twenties. He was up against some pretty heavy-duty people. After they discovered Natalie's body in the morning, Christopher Walken and Robert Wagner were taken away in a sheriff's helicopter back to the mainland and able to go home. They were barely even questioned.

Robert Wagner left Dennis to identify Natalie Wood's body. That's how close Dennis was with Natalie. He was told by Robert Wagner to say nothing, and "we'll have an attorney for you lined up when you get back to the mainland." Later that afternoon, Dennis was taken directly to Robert Wagner's house. So, Dennis was standing in Robert Wagner's bedroom and was told by an attorney, who Dennis knew was once connected with the mob, to not say anything. Another lawyer would have the paperwork ready for Dennis to sign the next day, which is what happened.

Then, Robert Wagner kept Dennis at his house for close to a year and kept a good eye on him. Dennis feared for his life, and death threats did come his way. As soon as he was able to break away from California, that's when he contacted me and said that he wanted to do something. He wanted to go to the authorities but, by that time, the authorities would not listen to him.

So, for all the times that we are asked, "Why did you wait 30 years?" The answer is this. "We did not wait 30 years. The authorities waited 30 years. The media waited 30 years." The mystery of Natalie's death festered in the news. People suspected things. There were a lot of mysteries surrounding Natalie's death. But if authorities would have listened to Dennis in the 1980s, that mystery may have been solved a long time ago.

Q. Did Robert Wagner and Natalie have fights that were physical?

A. No, they didn't. Dennis saw a very happy couple. When Dennis saw them married the first time around, there's a lot of information about that marriage out there now. I've had so many conversations with Natalie Wood's sister Lana Wood. Apparently, the first marriage broke up because Natalie had caught "RJ," Robert Wagner's nickname, supposedly in a compromising position with another man. She went running home and never went back to him. She just could not reconcile that betrayal that she felt.

Robert Wagner let Natalie take the brunt for that. It was said that she had fallen in love with Warren Beatty, her co-star in *Splendor in the Grass*. But that relationship hadn't started until Natalie and RJ were separated for a long time. Then, they divorced, both married someone else, and they each had a daughter.

Once again, Natalie's husband, Richard Gregson, from England, Natalie caught him cheating with the family secretary, and she left him. She came back to California. She had been living abroad, but then she divorced Richard Gregson.

THE SHIP'S CAPTAIN 253

Richard Gregson was a British agent, film producer, and screenwriter. He spent his early career working in America, alongside stars such as Robert Redford, Julie Christie, Alan Bates, and Gene Hackman and director John Schlesinger. He married the American actress Natalie Wood on May 30, 1969. The couple filed for divorce on August 4, 1971, and the divorce was finalized in April of the following year. Together they had one child, the actress Natasha Gregson Wagner, born 1970.[1]

But when she got back, she had bumped into RJ at a party, and they reconciled and remarried in 1972. Then, they had a daughter together. Robert Wagner's marriage to Marion Marshall, with who he had the daughter Katie, that marriage had ended before they had met up again.

After they had a daughter together, she accepted a movie offer for *Brainstorm*, and RJ was so upset with her because he wanted to be the breadwinner this time around. That's when the trouble started.

When Natalie decided to go away on location, he just wanted her home.

Robert Wagner told Dennis he was going to fly to North Carolina where Natalie was filming on location because Robert Wagner was sure that she was having an affair, and he wanted to catch her. But he visited her and came back, and everything seemed fine.

After *Brainstorm* was finished on location, Natalie and Christopher Walken still had a couple of studio scenes to do in Hollywood. So, Natalie was home for the Thanksgiving weekend. She invited Christopher Walken aboard their boat. It's what RJ and Natalie always did. When they had co-stars, they invited them aboard the boat. Sean Connery was aboard the boat when he made *Meteor* with her. George Seagull was as well when they made *Last Married Couple in America*. This was nothing unusual.

But this bothered Robert Wagner. Christopher Walken was the up-and-coming star of Hollywood. He was a New York-based actor with a quirkiness about him. A new feeling about him that Hollywood loved.

Natalie was thrilled to be working with him. She had no desire to flaunt her co-star in front of RJ. She simply invited him on the boat to do what they always did. It was holiday weekend, and she wanted to get some early Christmas shopping done. They left on Black Friday for the cruise. It was a rainy, miserable weekend, but Natalie insisted on still going. They went to Catalina Island, and that's when all hell broke loose.

Q. So, RJ was jealous of Christopher Walken?

A. Yes. He was very worried about it. He was probably jealous, thinking that he was this younger up and coming Hollywood star. He was probably jealous of Walken's instant career. Walken had won the Oscar for *The Deer Hunter* just a year before he started working with Natalie. Then, probably jealous because Walken was making a movie with Natalie.

There had been other times during their marriage where RJ had become jealous of her co-star. Like William Devane when Natalie made *From Here to Eternity*. There were episodes such as one time when they were at the Polo Club, and somebody made a comment towards Natalie, and RJ punched him in the face. There were times of RJ's jealousy, and he had a temper. Natalie didn't like it, and it seemed to happen when RJ drank. She was not happy with the way that RJ had been drinking that last year.

On this particular cruise to Catalina Island, it was the four of them – Natalie, RJ, Christopher Walken, and Dennis, the so-called Captain of the boat. Dennis more or less just maintained the boat. RJ was actually the boss and the Captain. That's why Dennis had to listen to him. So, they anchored at Avalon and moored at the Isthmus Island. They went to Avalon, where there are curios shops and trendy restaurants. RJ and Natalie went ashore and did some Christmas shopping, and

THE SHIP'S CAPTAIN 257

they had lunch on the island. Dennis stayed back on the boat and was making dinner for that night.

That evening after dinner, RJ had been drinking all day, and all of a sudden, he decided he wanted to move the boat to a different part of the island where there were only one restaurant and a diver's chamber, and that's it. Natalie didn't want to move the boat in the rain and the choppy waters at ten o'clock at night. RJ got angry. He started yelling. He went out and was pulling anchor. He told Dennis to start the engines. Natalie then asked Dennis to take her to shore.

RJ started to calm down and told Dennis to take her ashore and watch her that night. Dennis took Natalie ashore, and they got two rooms at the Pavilion Lodge. Dennis did stay in Natalie's room because she was very frightened. So, she asked Dennis to stay in her room.

The next morning Natalie tried to get a seaplane to get to the mainland. She called her sister, Lana, but could not get in touch with her, and there were no seaplanes flying. So, she decided to go back to the boat. Dennis did not want that. He considered this already the cruise from hell, and he tried to talk her out of it. But they went back to the boat.

Natalie made breakfast, and everything seemed like nothing happened the night before. RJ then decided that they were going to move the boat. So, they moved the boat to the quiet part of the island called "Two Harbors," where RJ wanted to go the night before.

Q. What was Christopher Walken doing the night before during the fight?

A. When he saw that RJ wanted to move the boat, he had just gone to his cabin to turn in for the night. During the little bit of arguing, Dennis had gone to Walken and asked him to help him out some by talking some sense into RJ. Walken preferred to stay out of it and even suggested to Dennis that he not get involved in any marital spat. Once they got to the Two Harbors and anchored the boat, Natalie told RJ that she and Christopher Walken were going to the restaurant. They would take a shore taxi there, and that RJ and Dennis could meet them for dinner. So, later that night, the four of them had cocktails and ate dinner ashore.

Q. Do we know how the dinner went? Were there any problems or arguments then?

A. It seemed that their dinner went fine. Dennis said RJ suddenly got into one of his deep dark moods again and wanted to leave the restaurant. Everyone was having a nice time and wanted to stay, but RJ insisted that they leave immediately.

Listen to the full interview with Marti Rulli on my website:

houseofmysteryradio/episodes/natalie-wood-marti-rulli

---

1. https://en.wikipedia.org/wiki/Richard_Gregson

The Hollywood Sister
INTERVIEW WITH LANA WOOD

Lana Wood was born Svetlana Gurdin on March 1, 1946, and is an American actress and film producer. She played Sandy Webber on the TV series *Peyton Place*, and Plenty O'Toole in the James Bond film *Diamonds Are Forever*. Her sister was film star Natalie Wood.[1]

Lana had made it very public that she believed that Robert Wagner was responsible for Natalie Wood's death by asking him on film to tell her the truth. This was the natural follow up for an interview in 2018.

Q. What was the relationship like between Robert Wagner and Natalie Wood at the time of her death?

A. Natalie was working. It was a time of change for her because she was concerned about getting roles, working, and finding the right roles to do. She was prepared to go back into acting more or less full time, certainly with a complete heart. Because she had already felt she had established her kids, and everything was going correctly, so she could continue with her career again.

How RJ felt about that? I don't know. You could probably answer that just about as well as I could with the male ego. It's tough when we've got one person more successful than the other, especially when it's a male and female. That always enters into it. It's something that is, I think, just a part of how things have been ingrained in a woman's role. So, I don't think that he was terrifically happy. So, it wasn't as though their relationship was bad at that time, but it was undergoing a change.

Q. Now, they had been married before, then divorced, then married again, correct?

A. Yes, indeed.

Q. Natalie's demeanor prior to that night, did she seem to be stressed? How was she acting?

A. No, not at all. She was in the middle of doing a film with Christopher Walken, so she was happy about that. They had just taken the holiday off. The film was not completed, but they had stopped filming for the holidays. She was feeling good and very positive about what the future would bring.

Q. Now, she was afraid of the water. Was going out on the boat something that was common for her?

A. Well, you know it was RJ's love. He just loved going out on the boat. She tried to make it as homey as possible. She enjoyed it to an extent. Natalie was more than afraid of water. She was terrified by it. Obviously, we had talked about it with my mom and Natalie. She was terrified of dark water because when my mom was growing up, she was born in Russia and raised in China, she had her fortune told. This woman actually told her that she would have a child who would be world-famous and beloved by all. But she saw death by drowning in deep, dark water. My mom was kind enough to share that information with us, and it was something that always stayed with Natalie. It didn't bother me much because I just didn't believe in stuff like that. But it troubled Natalie, always. She didn't know how to swim. She wouldn't swim in her own pool even. She wouldn't go in it.

Q. Now, that night that they were on the boat, I believe the name of the boat was "The Splendour."

A. Yes.

Q. That night, who was she with on the boat?

A. She had invited her co-star Christopher Walken and the man who sort of ran the boat and kept things ship-shape. RJ gave him the title of Captain. Dennis Davern and RJ. That was it.

Q. I have read several statements written by Christopher Walken and the boat's Captain Dennis Davern, and both of them said there was an argument between Robert Wagner and Natalie Wood. What do you know about that?

A. There were actually two fights. The night before, Natalie got so upset she wanted to leave the boat and come home. What she did was ask Dennis to stay with her in a motel on the island. She didn't even spend the night on the boat. She didn't want to be there. She wanted to come home. Then, lo and behold, in the morning, she changed her mind and decided to go see if she could make things better. So, she went back.

That was the night a big fight ensued that evidently started when they went out to dinner on the island. Then, they carried it over to the boat. It was not a happy evening. RJ had become so furious that he became violent, and picked up a wine bottle and literally broke the wine bottle. Then, he was threatening with the wine bottle. Bad stuff going on. Very, very bad stuff.

Christopher, at that time, said he was not going to get involved. He left and went to his room and went to bed. Natalie said that she had had enough and stormed off to their cabin and got ready for bed. She took a sleeping pill, got in her nightgown, and was ready for bed. RJ stormed in after drinking more and continued the fight.

What's odd is, people say, "Oh well, that he couldn't, he didn't." It's odd because I don't know if you've ever seen the layout of the "Splendour?"

Q. No.

A. The bedroom doors open directly onto the rear deck. It's not a step up. It's not a climb around. They open directly onto the rear deck.

According to Dennis, who I certainly believe, particularly now that they have a new coroner with better methods and a little bit more thorough, two people were fighting violently. First, in the room, and Dennis went to the door and knocked on it, and asked if everything was okay. RJ told him to mind his own business and shut the door on him. But according to Dennis, RJ appeared very disheveled and out of control.

The fight was carried out and onto the back of the boat. At this point, Dennis started to walk around to go to the back of the boat because he heard them continuing to fight. He turned up the music because RJ was very concerned about anybody hearing anything. It was for privacy. So, Dennis turned up the music, walked to the back of the boat, and only saw RJ standing there. Dennis asked where Natalie was, and RJ said that she was gone.

Dennis asked, "What do you mean she's gone? Is she overboard? Do you want me to turn on the lights?" RJ wouldn't let him turn on the lights, call the coastguard or anything. They continued drinking. It doesn't make sense.

You've got two people on the back of the boat, and then suddenly, there's one. Then, RJ said some very stupid and cruel things that couldn't be further from the truth of who Natalie is, which angers me equally. He said, "Oh, she probably went off to a party because she was that kind of woman." What? In a nightgown, with wool socks, and her face scrubbed clean. I don't think so. Natalie wouldn't go to the mailbox unless she was fully dressed. She obviously didn't go and pick up her own mail, but you know what I'm saying.

Natalie was a star, and she was always concerned about how people would perceive her, how she looked, and what she needed to do. She was very fan conscious and conscious of her reputation. So, it made no sense to me that there were two people standing on the back of the boat, then suddenly there was only one.

Q. From what you're saying, Lana, it sounds like RJ was pretty calm through it all?

A. That I don't know. But he certainly didn't seem concerned, let's put it that way. I mean, he didn't want to put on the lights or to call anyone.

Q. Did Robert Wagner normally have a temper? Was it something that was common, or was it rare?

A. That I wouldn't know because that goes on behind closed doors. I really can't answer that honestly, so I won't even try.

Q. It's my understanding that the ship's Captain, Dennis Davern, at one time actually lied about the story. But later changed his story?

A. Yes, he did lie. He did what RJ told him to. RJ told him what to say. He told Christopher what to say. He said, "We all got to be on the same page. It'll make it easier for everybody." He literally told Dennis what to say, and Dennis went along with it. Christopher just clammed up. He didn't speak for a very long time.

Another thing that bothered me was why RJ didn't go to be next to his wife when her body was found? Why didn't he identify her? No, he sent Dennis. He and Christopher left in a helicopter to go back home and left Dennis there.

Q. I know that there is a new Medical Examiner on the case, and there was a new 10-page amendment to the autopsy report. It indicates that there are some changes and new information. Can you tell us what that is?

A. Well, they say that the bruising all over her body was that of someone who was being abused and not of someone who was bumping up against a rubber dingy. She also had a bruise mark in the center of her throat. She had too many bruises. It was ridiculous. They were all over and indicative of a fight.

Natalie was teeny tiny. She was 5 foot 2 inches and weighed 105 pounds.

The coroner also said that she had a full bladder and that the seawater found in her lungs was actually seafoam and a small amount of water. So, she was quite possibly unconscious or dead when she went into the water.

Then, you had Thomas Noguchi, who did the first autopsy, and he didn't do "shades of grey," he just did "black or white." You know big celebrities were involved, and he did a very quick autopsy, a minimal amount of anything. He said that he didn't do a thorough examination. He didn't look at her nail clippings. He didn't do a rape kit. There were a lot of things that just weren't done.

Q. I read that she had an abrasion on her left cheek. Is that true?

A. Yes. She also had one on her forehead, her legs were bruised, and her arms were bruised. And, as I said, the center of her throat, too, was also bruised. They were all fresh bruises.

Q. I've noticed that Robert Wagner has now been named a person of interest in the case back in February 2018. That sort of changes things, doesn't it?

A. Yes, it does. It changes a great many things. Lieutenant Corina from the Sheriff's Department has held conferences and asked if there's anybody who saw anything at all. Particularly seeing her being hit or something. Any little piece of anything that they saw to please come forward.

They have two new witnesses that are unwilling. They didn't come forward then, and they didn't come forward this time. They were actually trapped into making statements, and they told the truth. So, he wants anything and everything. We still don't know who the two new witnesses are or what information they have given. But the two detectives on the case that keep me informed say they feel they have enough now to arrest Robert Wagner. But it was the District Attorney who said no, that they need more.

Q. I also understand that they changed the cause of death on her autopsy to "drowning and other undetermined factors." Is that true?

A. Yes, that's correct, because it was not simply drowning. The new coroner said that she was already unconscious or already dead when she hit the water. And that things just don't add up.

Q. What has Robert Wagner ever said about the case?

A. RJ has never spoken about it again. He just spoke about that night, and that was it. He has refused to talk to them. Even the two detectives that are still on the case from homicide went to his home in Colorado, and they were not allowed in. He's refused to speak to them every time they've tried. Then, his attorney comes out and says that Robert Wagner has always been cooperative with the police. No, he has not. He spoke to them on the day it happened but has not spoken to them since.

My feeling is if you have nothing to hide, why wouldn't you want to speak to them? Even if it's simply clearing your own name. Where is the love? Where is the caring? It simply isn't there.

Q. One of the other things I noticed that was different on the autopsy report was, "How Natalie ended up in the water was not clearly established." That statement really stood out to me. Before, it was an accidental drowning. Now, they have realized that there's something else to this. She may have not just slipped into the water or off the dingy.

A. Yes, it is significant. We have better methods now, and people that are doing their jobs now.

Q. What are your thoughts on Robert Wagner?

A. I just wish he would be a man and come out and tell the truth. I'm not in judgment of him. I was not there. I don't know what happened. But I know these things are possible for anybody. I don't feel it was premeditated. I don't think it was planned. I don't believe all of that nonsense that comes out. I just deal with the facts. But I can't believe that he wouldn't want to tell the truth. He blames everybody. He blamed Dennis Davern and anybody that he possibly can. Even I've come under fire, and I haven't done anything. I'm not dealing with suppositions.

I know my sister better than I know myself because I can view her in a different way than how I view myself. She would not do any of the things that he first claimed she did. I don't know. You know it's possible for anybody at any time to cross that line. As I said, I'm not judging him. I just want truth and honesty. He needs to stop making other people the "fall guy."

I feel for her children. It's so ugly to accept that this is what happened that you don't want to. I had my head in the sand for years. It was always nibbling at me, but I never said anything. I never pursued anything. I just knew that Natalie would never behave as he said. He was extremely jealous. He was accusing Christopher Walken of having an affair with Natalie as well.

I just wish he would tell the truth. Then what happens after that is not up to me. I'm sorry that will hurt her kids even more. I don't feel any anger or love for RJ. He was not my pal. If I was in their house, it was to be with Natalie. You know, when she announced at an impromptu dinner that she was remarrying RJ, the minute I could, I grabbed her and asked her what she was doing. She said sometimes it's better to be with the devil you know than the devil you don't. I don't accept that. I would have accepted that she still loved him, but better to be with the devil you know, no.

Listen to the full interview with Lana Wood on my website:

www.alanrwarren.com/hom-podcast-episodes/episode/1a03b723/lana-wood-natalie-wood-death

1. https://en.wikipedia.org/wiki/Lana_Wood

PART V
Princess Diana

Diana, Princess of Wales, was born Diana Frances Spencer on July 1, 1961. She was a member of the British royal family. She was the first wife of Charles, Prince of Wales, the heir apparent to the British throne, and was the mother of Prince William and Prince Harry.

Diana was born into the British nobility and grew up close to the royal family on their Sandringham estate. The youngest daughter of John Spencer, 8th Earl Spencer, and Frances Shand Kydd, she was strongly affected by their divorce in 1967.

Diana came to prominence in 1981 upon her engagement to Prince Charles, the eldest son of Queen Elizabeth II, after a brief courtship. Their wedding took place at St Paul's Cathedral in 1981 and made her Princess of Wales, a role in which she was enthusiastically received by the public. As Princess of Wales, Diana undertook royal duties on behalf of the Queen and represented her at functions across the Commonwealth realms. She was celebrated in the media for her unconventional approach to charity work.

Considered to be very photogenic, she was a leader of fashion in the 1980s and 1990s. Media attention and public mourning were extensive after her death in a car crash in a Paris tunnel in 1997 and subsequent televised funeral. Her legacy has had a deep impact on the royal family and British society.[1]

Death

On August 31, 1997, Diana died in a car crash in the Pont de l'Alma tunnel in Paris while the driver was fleeing the paparazzi. The crash also resulted in the deaths of her companion Dodi Fayed and the driver, Henri Paul, who was the acting security manager of the Hôtel Ritz Paris. Diana's bodyguard, Trevor Rees-Jones, survived the crash.

On September 6th, the televised funeral was watched by a British television audience that peaked at 32.10 million, which was one of the United Kingdom's highest viewing figures ever. Millions more watched the event around the world.

The initial French judicial investigation concluded that the crash was caused by Paul's intoxication, reckless driving, speeding 65 m.p.h., and effects of prescription drugs. In February 1998, Mohamed Al-Fayed, owner of the Paris Ritz where Paul had worked, publicly said the crash had been planned and accused MI6 and the Duke of Edinburgh.

An inquest that started in London in 2004 and continued in 2007–08 attributed the crash to grossly negligent driving by Paul and to the pursuing paparazzi, who forced Paul to speed into the tunnel.

On April 7, 2008, the jury returned a verdict of unlawful killing. On the day after the inquest's final verdict, Al-Fayed announced that he would end his 10-year campaign to establish that the tragedy was murder. He said he did so for the sake of Diana's children.

In 1999, after the submission of a Freedom of Information Act request filed by the Internet news service apbonline.com, it was revealed that Diana had been placed under surveillance by the National Security Agency until her death. The organization kept a top-secret file on her containing more than 1,000 pages. The contents of Diana's NSA file cannot be disclosed because of national security concerns. The NSA officials insisted Diana was not a target of massive, worldwide electronic eavesdropping infrastructure. Despite multiple inquiries for the files to be declassified – with one of the notable ones being filed by Mohamed Al-Fayed – the NSA has refused to release the documents.

In 2008, Ken Wharfe, a former bodyguard of Diana, claimed that her scandalous conversations with James Gilbey were recorded by the GCHQ, which intentionally released them on a "loop." People close to Diana believed the action was intended to defame her. Wharfe said Diana herself believed that members of the royal family were all being monitored, though he also stated that the main reason for it could be the potential threats of the IRA.[2]

---

1. https://en.wikipedia.org/wiki/Diana,_Princess_of_Wales
2. Diana, Princess of Wales - Newikis. https://newikis.com/en/Diana,_Princess_of_Wales

John Morgan

INTERVIEW WITH JOHN MORGAN

John Morgan, who is based in Brisbane, Australia, is an investigative writer with a diploma in journalism. Since 2005, he has carried out extensive full-time research into the events surrounding the deaths of Diana, Princess of Wales, and Dodi Fayed. John viewed it as a huge injustice to the memory of Princess Diana.

The 2007 book, *Cover-up of a Royal Murder*, was the result of his subsequent investigation into the "Paget Report," documenting the 2007 inquest the jury had prevented the public from seeing. The *Diana Inquest* series of books is the result of his thorough research and investigation into the facts of the case.

John went on to closely follow and analyze the proceedings and transcripts of the London inquest into the deaths of Princess Diana and Dodi Fayed. In 2010, he received over 500 documents from within the official British police investigation, Operation Paget.

The John Morgan interview was in 2014.

Q. How did you get interested in the death of Princess Diana?

A. I got interested in the case of Princess Diana after there was a letter published in 2003, which was a note from Diana to her butler, that predicted she could die in an orchestrated car crash. I saw that handwritten note, which was published in the newspapers all around the world, and within two years, she actually did die as she predicted in the letter.

The Princess of Wales wrote to her former butler, Paul Burrell, saying her life was at its "most dangerous" phase, the *Daily Mirror* reported. It quotes the letter as saying: "XXXX is planning 'an accident' in my car, brake failure and serious head injury in order to make the path clear for Charles to marry."[1]

That was a very significant piece of evidence, I thought. In 2006, I retired and decided I could write a book and decided I would do a bit of research on that crash. In 2006, when the police investigation was completed in December of 2006, I had already done about 18 months of research on what had taken place.

After the police report was put online, I printed out all 800 pages and read it. I then realized that the police investigation had not really been an investigation and appeared to be more interested in trying to cover it up. There were so many errors in that report as I already knew a lot about it.

The police investigation finished in December of 2006, and the inquest started ten months later in October 2007. During that time, I published a book about the police report, and Mohamed Al-Fayed distributed it to the lawyers at the inquest. I got feedback from a lot of the lawyers who said they used the book in the inquest.

Mohamed Al-Fayed is an Egyptian-born businessman whose residence and chief business interests have been in the United Kingdom since the late 1960s. Fayed's business interests include ownership of Hôtel Ritz Paris and formerly Harrods Department Store. Fayed famously had a son, Dodi, from his first marriage to Samira Khashoggi from 1954 to 1956. Dodi was in a romantic relationship with Diana, Princess of Wales, when they both died in a car crash in Paris in 1997.

From February 1998, Al-Fayed maintained that the crash was a result of a conspiracy and later contended that the crash was orchestrated by MI6 on the instructions of Prince Philip, Duke of Edinburgh.[2]

Al-Fayed first claimed that the Princess was pregnant to the *Daily Express* in May 2001 and that he was the only person who had been told of this news. Witnesses at the inquest who said the Princess was not pregnant, and could not have been, were part of the conspiracy, according to Al-Fayed.

Fayed's testimony at the inquest was roundly condemned in the press as being farcical. Members of the British Government's Intelligence and Security Committee accused Fayed of turning the inquest into a 'circus' and called for it to be ended maturely. Lawyers representing Al-Fayed later accepted at the inquest that there was no direct evidence that either the Duke of Edinburgh or MI6 had been involved in any murder conspiracy involving Diana or Dodi. His claims that the crash was a result of a conspiracy were dismissed by a French judicial investigation, but Fayed appealed against this verdict. The British "Operation Paget," a Metropolitan police inquiry that concluded in 2006, also found no evidence of a conspiracy. To Al-Fayed made 175 conspiracy claims. In 2013, Fayed's wealth was estimated at US$1.4 billion, making him the 1,031st richest person in the world.[3]

As the transcripts of the inquest came out, I would read through and study them, and I wrote a series of six volumes based on what was in the inquest transcripts, but also the police reports. In 2010, I received a huge batch of documents that were from the British police investigation, and there were very critical documents about the case, and none of them had been shown to the jury at the inquest. I published a lot of those documents, including the post-mortem reports for Princess Diana and Dodi Fayed, none of which were shown to the jury either while investigating the cause of death. One of the things that's very interesting is that the verdict of that inquest jury was quite different from what the police investigation had concluded.

Dodi Fayed was an Egyptian film producer and the son of billionaire Mohamed Al-Fayed. He was the romantic partner of Diana, Princess of Wales, when they both died in a car crash in Paris in 1997. In July 1997, Fayed became romantically involved with Diana, Princess of Wales. Earlier that summer, Fayed had become engaged to an American model, Kelly Fisher, and had bought a house in Malibu, California, for himself and Fisher with money from his father. Fisher subsequently claimed Fayed had jilted her for Diana and announced that she was filing a breach of contract suit against him, claiming he had led her emotionally all the way up to the altar and abandoned her when they were almost there. He threw her love away in a callous way with no regard for her whatsoever. She dropped the lawsuit shortly after Fayed's death.[4]

Naturally, there was a French police investigation that started on the day of the crash. In 1999, they produced their results that stated the crash was caused by the driver, Henri Paul, who was drunk. The British police investigation that came out in 2006 also said that it was caused by the driver, Henri Paul, who was drunk and speeding. So, it was a very similar finding to the French investigation.

But the inquest jury's verdict was quite different. It was unlawful killing by the driver of the Mercedes, Henri Paul, but also by unknown following vehicles, which have not been identified. But they were not paparazzi. So, quite different from what the police had concluded.

Henri Paul was the driver of the Mercedes W140, in which Diana, Princess of Wales, died on August 31, 1997. As Deputy Head of Security at the Hôtel Ritz Paris, Paul had been off duty that evening but was called back to drive Diana and Dodi Fayed to their apartment. The car crashed at high speed in the Pont de l'Alma tunnel, with only bodyguard Trevor Rees-Jones surviving. British and French police investigations put the blame largely on Paul for being impaired by alcohol and later driving recklessly.

On the night of August 31, 1997, Paul was under the influence of alcohol and tried to elude paparazzi photographers at high speed estimated at over double the 50 kilometers per hour speed limit, when the Mercedes S280 he was driving crashed into a column supporting the Pont de l'Alma tunnel in Paris. Paul's blood alcohol content level was subsequently found to be between 1.73 g/L and 1.75 g/L or 0.17% mass/vol. A figure more than three times the threshold for drunk driving as defined under French law. Paul's parents dispute the authenticity and the accuracy of the test results, as does Dodi's father, Mohamed Al-Fayed. There have been many conspiracy theories surrounding the car crash.[5]

> The establishment didn't really get it past the jury, even though the true finding would have been murder. The jury was not unanimous. It was 9-2. There were two jurors who did not conclude unlawful killing. They concluded murder.

French Investigation

Friends of Henri Paul testified in statements to the French police that he did not have a remarkably high tolerance for alcohol and was seen on social occasions to drink for several hours while showing obvious signs of drunkenness. In her statement to French police, his medical doctor, Dominique Mélo, who was also a friend, explained: "Henri drank like everyone else, but not to excess. He did not have the clinical stigmata or the behavior of a chronic alcoholic," she explained further.

Paul's doctor testified that in the two years leading up to his death, he had depressive episodes about the break-up of a long-term relationship and had sometimes taken to drinking at home outside a social context. She believed he was not alcohol-dependent, but she was worried that he might become so, and in about June 1996, she prescribed him the anti-depressant Prozac and an anti-alcoholism medication Aotal. Traces of the anti-depressants were found in post-mortem examinations of his blood. The inquest revealed that the autopsy also found Paul's liver to be normal with no indicating signs of problems connected with alcoholism.[6]

British Investigation

Operation Paget investigated the reliability of the post-mortem examinations using DNA comparison of the disputed blood sample by comparing a DNA profile from it with Paul's mother's DNA profile. The test produced a result that there was a maternal relationship between the two profiles to a probability of 99.9997%. The level of carbon monoxide in this blood sample was attributed to the area of the body it was taken from, to his living in a built-up urban area, and smoking of small cigars in the hours leading up to his death.

It was disclosed that in November 2006, John Stevens had a meeting with Paul's parents and told them that their son was not drunk and was found to have indisputably had two alcoholic drinks. This was verified by bodyguards Trevor Rees-Jones and Kieran Wingfield, two barmen in the bar, the till records from the hotel bar, and a drink bill. Five weeks later, the report stated that Paul was twice over the British drink-drive limit and three times over the French limit.

An expert cited in the report estimated that Paul had drunk the equivalent of ten small glasses of Ricard pastis, his favorite aperitif, before driving. At the British inquest in February 2008, Stevens denied "deliberately misleading" Paul's parents and explained the apparent contradiction in his statements by saying that Paul did not meet the standard definition of being drunk, which is dependent on observable physical behavior. He was though clearly "under the influence" of alcohol and unfit to drive.

An unexplained prescription-only drug called albendazole used to treat worm infestations was also found in hair samples from Paul. This drug is said to be commonly given to homeless people living on the streets. Paul's doctor denies prescribing this drug to Paul.

Q. So, are you saying that the police covered up that it was murder? Or, are you saying that it was just really bad police work?

A. No, it was intentionally covered up. One of the things was if you studied how the investigation was done, there are elements of them trying to find the truth. I think it was lower-level officers who were working on the case. Some of them were genuine in interviewing witnesses and were trying to establish what happened.

But yes, the police at the top was covering up, so they had to reach a conclusion that it was not murder. It's interesting, there's the stuff that indicates murder, and they drew these conclusions that it was an accident. It was quite easy when I did this book to show, well, that this evidence indicates murder. Yet they conclude it was an accident, a contradiction to what the evidence was. Very strange.

Q. How were the police and other officials towards you when you were investigating this case?

A. I haven't had any direct overtures from the establishment or against me. There was a lot of indirect stuff on the internet, but nothing direct. Nobody has given me a death threat or anything like that.

Q. Do you think the car accident was planned out ahead of time?

A. Yeah, it was a planned operation. Diana was under surveillance, so they were monitoring her when she was traveling around with Dodi and various trips that she was making. There was a phone call that

Dodi made to the Ritz in Paris, which was owned by his father, on the 18th of August 1997. So, that was two weeks before. During that phone call, it was clear from anyone monitoring it that there was no doubt Dodi's phone calls were being monitored as well as Diana's. But there was a very clear statement that they would be traveling to Paris at the end of August.

So, basically, anyone that was part of the operation, which would have been units of the M16, would have been aware that the couple would be traveling to Paris at the end of August. And they had two weeks to organize the details of what they were going to do. It was an extremely well-planned operation. I think it was done with the help of the French intelligence and also the CIA. You can see the units are planning right through the operation. They knew in advance what they were going to do to cover it up – things like nailing it on the paparazzi and also on the drunk driver.

If you walked down the streets of London and asked people, "Who killed Diana," a lot of people would say the paparazzi. The other thing they might say is the driver because he was drunk. So, there are just two things in most people's minds, and they are both erroneous.

But these things were worked out before the crash, and you can see the evidence of it. Things like Henri Paul, who was working for intelligence, had no idea of what he was involved in. He had no idea that they were about to kill Diana. He probably thought the things he was doing was helping to protect her. One of the things and he was paid very well as there was a lot of money that went into his account, was Henri Paul acting as head of security for the hotel. The hotel was trying to secure the well-being of the guests, and Diana and Dodi were VIP guests. Yet Henri Paul was going out to the paparazzi and telling them when they were going to be coming out. He made about five trips in total out to the paparazzi, telling them, "They're not going to be very long."

So, why does anyone do that? It wasn't for the interest of the couple as they didn't want to be hounded by the paparazzi. The reason he was doing it was to make sure the paparazzi didn't go home as it was getting towards midnight, and they might have thought that the couple was just staying overnight, so there was no point in waiting outside. He was making sure that the paparazzi were staying, and he was getting paid to do that. That's why when the couple left the hotel, the paparazzi were still there, and they followed the Mercedes. They were on scooters and small cars, and they began the chase.

Once they got onto the expressway and heading towards the tunnel, they practically had no chance of keeping up. The witnesses who saw what happened on the expressway all say they saw several motorbikes surrounding the Mercedes. These were large dark motorbikes, and a couple of them had two passengers on them. The motorbikes were also taking flash photos as the car headed toward the tunnel. Basically, what I call "fake paparazzi." They were pretending to be paparazzi. So this was the whole thing, people that saw the motorbikes probably thought paparazzi as well. Then you've got to ask who was driving the motorbikes. None of the drivers on the motorbikes have been identified.

Even though the jury decided that there was unlawful chase by the motorbikes, when the inquest was completed, there was no attempt by any of the authorities in France or England to establish the identity of those motorbike riders.

They had been forced into the crash through surrounding motorbikes, and there was also a flash strobe light to the driver in the tunnel. If that were a normal person that this was done to, those motorbikes were the cause of the crash and unidentified, immediately following there would be a police investigation to establish who those motorbike riders were. That never occurred, as it's all part of the coverup.

Q. Was there a detail there that was assigned to protect Diana?

A. The royals do, but Diana wasn't a royal at the time, as she had been removed from the royal family a year earlier. Even when she was a royal in 1994, she had requested that her guard be withdrawn. She was no longer under day-to-day bodyguard protection from the police.

Q. You talk about the post-crash medical treatment of Diana. What's your opinion of it?

A. She survived the crash. So, when the crash occurred, it crashed under the third pillar of the tunnel at 60 miles an hour. The two people who were on the driver's side, Henri Paul, the driver in the front, and Dodi Fayed, the passenger sitting behind him in the back, both died instantly. The two people on the passenger side, Trevor Rees-Jones, the bodyguard was in the front, he's still alive, and Princess Diana in the back. She initially survived. Both of those people on the passenger side survived.

Trevor Rees-Jones is a German-born British bodyguard of Princess Diana. On August 31, 1997, Rees-Jones was seriously injured in the crash that resulted in the death of Diana, Princess of Wales. The Princess's boyfriend, Dodi Fayed, and the driver of the car, Henri Paul, were pronounced dead at the scene. Rees-Jones was the only survivor. Rees suffered severe brain and chest injuries, and every bone in his face was broken. He spent ten days in a coma. His face was reconstructed from family photographs by maxillofacial surgeon Luc Chikhani, using about 150 pieces of titanium to hold the bones together and recreate the original shape. Within a year, his face was nearly back to normal. Hospital care costs were paid by Dodi's father, Mohamed Al-Fayed, Rees-Jones's employer at the time of the crash, and the rest by the British National Health Service.

At first, it was widely rumored that Rees-Jones had lost his tongue in the crash, but this was untrue. He underwent a 10-hour operation to restore his jaw to a normal condition. Rees-Jones returned to Britain on October 3, 1997, having spent a month in the hospital. At the time, he was able to communicate only by whispering and writing down answers. He resigned from his job as a bodyguard on May 19, 1998. Al-Fayed was reported as saying that his job would be available if he wished to return.

Rees-Jones wrote a book, published in 2000 and titled *The Bodyguard's Story: Diana, the Crash, and the Sole Survivor,* about his experiences, with the help of ghostwriter Moira Johnston. The book reconstructed the events from Rees-Jones's partial memories and those of his family and friends. He decided to write the book because many bizarre stories had circulated about the crash and because his former employer, Al-Fayed, had accused him of not doing his job properly.[7]

The ambulance and the medical treatment are really the things that took her life. Immediately after the crash at 12:21 a.m., there were two doctors that ran the base overnight. One of them was asleep, and the other one was Doctor Arnaud Derossi, who was taking the calls. He allocated an ambulance to the crash, which was Doctor Jean-Marc Martino, who didn't arrive until

12:47 a.m. However, the hospital he was dispatched from was only 2.3 kilometers away. So, he took a hell of a long time to get to the crash. It took 13 minutes to travel 2.3 kilometers.

Intelligence agencies use people as agents to do their work. They use people from all sorts of walks of life. People can have their career as a doctor, but they could also be working as an agent. It could be your next-door neighbor. That's how they operate. The people have a normal job, and then they'll also be working for intelligence part-time. And they'll get a lot of money for what they do.

Both Doctors, Derossi and Marino, were working for intelligence. It took them 43 minutes to deliver Diana to the hospital. So, there was a very long period of time when she was in their care. At the inquest, one of the issues was that the healthcare system is different in Paris, and it is different, that's true.

In the U.S., it is called "scoop and run," when a person is in a car crash and injured, the ambulance rushes to the scene and picks up the victim, and rushes them to the hospital. In Paris and in France, what they have is a system that there's a doctor onboard the ambulance, and they have more equipment in the ambulance. So, the ambulance arrives at the crash scene, and they try to stabilize the patient. Then, they take them to the hospital.

But even in France, there are times when they will rush the person to the hospital. It depends on what the perception of the injuries is. If you've got a patient who is in Diana's situation, considering what she had been through, she had been in a 60 mile an hour car crash and wasn't wearing a seat belt, so her body was swung around 180 degrees, and she ended up on the floor with her back against the back of the front seat, and her legs up on the back seat. The thing is, doctors know that when you're involved in a crash like that, there could be some sort of internal injuries. It took 20 minutes from when the ambulance arrived to get her out of the car. Then, she got into the ambulance at 1:06 a.m., which was already

43 minutes after the crash. Once in the ambulance, they examined her. They saw she had bruises on the chest, and her blood pressure had dropped to 70. So, they knew at that stage that she had an injury they could not deal with in the ambulance. And that's the issue.

We have the transcripts from the base, and even they were asking the ambulance when they were leaving. The ambulance stayed in the tunnel for one hour and one minute. The other thing that you can see from the transcripts is that Doctor Derossi, who is the one phoning the base, said nothing to the base about Diana having a thoracic trauma. So, they didn't have a cardiac expert on hand to deal with Diana. If they had told the base that there was a thoracic trauma, then the base would have told the hospital what they needed.

Thoracic trauma is broadly categorized by mechanism into blunt or penetrating trauma. The most common cause of blunt chest trauma is motor vehicle collisions, which account for up to

80% of injuries. Other causes include falls, vehicles striking pedestrians, acts of violence, and blast injuries. Many patients with chest trauma die after reaching the hospital. Less than 10% of all blunt thoracic injuries require a thoracotomy, and many potentially life-threatening conditions can be relieved by simple procedures, such as chest tube insertion. Thus, many cases of traumatic deaths due to chest injury may be prevented by prompt diagnosis and a standardized therapeutic approach in the emergency room.

> The other thing was that just before the ambulance got to the hospital, they stopped. There were two gentlemen who witnessed it. They witnessed a rocking ambulance. They also witnessed the driver coming out of the front and going into the back. They already had three people in the back. They had the doctor and two student interns. So, they ended up with four people in the back. This was just 500 yards from the hospital, and they never gave an

explanation for why they stopped for five minutes.

The witnesses saw the ambulance rocking, so what were they doing? They said that they stopped the ambulance to give a cardiac massage and to increase the fluids because they thought that she might have a cardiac arrest. But she never had a cardiac arrest at that time.

When she got to the hospital, she only survived for another six minutes. So, the focus must be on what happened in the ambulance. Why did she die right after arriving at the hospital?

Q. Trevor Reese-Jones survived the crash and claims that he has no real memory of the accident. What are your thoughts on that?

A. Yes. He's changed his statement a few times. His evidence is very unreliable. I think that there are issues with the bodyguards – both Rees and the bodyguard at the hotel. The bodyguards were also at the same table as Henri Paul when he was drinking alcohol, so they shouldn't have allowed him to drive. They never did that. They both claimed that he was drinking pineapple juice, but they knew he was drinking Ricard. They both would have lost their jobs if they admitted they knew that Henri Paul was drinking the day before they left the hotel.

The whole idea of Henri driving the car was a bit unusual anyway because he had never actually driven during his 11 years at the hotel. When he went out to the airport that day, that was the first time he had ever driven for the hotel. He only had the luggage with him on the trip from the airport to the hotel. When he had the crash in the tunnel, that was the first time he had ever driven guests for the hotel.

I haven't studied the amnesia part yet of Trevor Rees-Jones, but it's something I need to do. The indication is that he may not have lost his memory because there's evidence from one of the housekeepers of his apartments in London. She said that she had spoken to Rees-Jones, and he told her not too long after the crash that if his memory came back, he would be in trouble.

Q. What more can you tell us about the driver Henri Paul?

A. He worked for the hotel, but the hotel was owned by Dodi's father, Mohamed Al-Fayed.

Q. But Mohamed Al-Fayed believes that his son, Dodi, and Diana were murdered and is offering a reward to find out the truth. Therefore, Henri Paul's boss didn't know that Paul was involved?

A. Yes, that's right. They have a different angle because they say that there's no way Henri Paul worked for intelligence. But the evidence that Henri Paul worked for intelligence is very strong. It's pretty standard these days that in these high-class hotels, people working in their security department also works for intelligence, simply because intelligence has an interest in people that visit high-class hotels. But Henri Paul was receiving much more money than his wage the hotel was paying him. He had 17 bank accounts, and he had intelligence contacts in his address book. So, he was definitely working for intelligence.

Q. So who actually wanted her dead? Who is the one that made the order?

A. The evidence indicates that there are two motives. First, there's the involvement in the Anti-Landmine campaign. She had been to Angola in January 1997, and she had received a death threat over the phone from the Minister of the Armed Forces in the UK, Nickolas Soames.

Diana became embroiled in political controversy after fronting a Red Cross campaign to bring in an international ban on landmines at a time when the British government wanted an exemption for its forces.

Nicholas Soames, Tory MP for Mid-Sussex, has been a friend of Prince Charles since they were both boys. He went on television in November

1995 to denounce Diana as paranoid when she complained about people in the Prince's camp being out to get her. Soames then threatened Diana six months before her death and warned her to stop meddling in a controversy over landmines. Diana's friend Simone Simmons had listened in on a telephone conversation at the Princess's invitation in February 1997 and heard the then Armed Forces Minister warn her "accidents can happen." But Soames told an inquest that he had never made a threatening phone call to her or ever discussed the landmines issue with her. "It's a really grotesque suggestion," he said. Michael Mansfield, QC, cross-examining Soames on behalf of Mohamed Al-Fayed, told him that he had a very distinctive voice and that Ms. Simmons was sure it was he who made the threatening phone call.[8]

> Then, in August, she went on another trip. This time to Bosnia. That was in the same month that she died. That trip was also part of her anti-landmines campaign, where she made a major speech about landmines. The fact is that Diana was a humanitarian,

and if she had gotten the landmines banned, she would have moved onto something else.

The other motive technically involved Mohamed Al-Fayed, who was a longtime family friend of her father. In June of 1997, he offered her a holiday in his villa in the South of France, and she accepted that. But it wasn't just her that was going to be going on this holiday. She was going to be taking Prince William and Prince Harry. Now, Prince William was going to be the next King of England. The trip caused concern in the British establishment because Mohamed Al-Fayed was looked on as a man of ill repute. Just earlier that year, he had been involved in the "Cash-for-Questions" scandal with the government of the UK. So, he was looked upon as quite involved in the change of party. The royals were thought to have had a hand in this too.

In 1994, in what became known as the "cash-for-questions affair," Mohammed Fayed revealed the names of MPs he had paid to ask questions in parliament on his behalf, but who had failed to declare their fees. It saw the Conservative MPs Neil Hamilton and Tim Smith leave the government in disgrace, and a Committee on Standards in Public Life established to prevent such corruption from occurring again.

Fayed also revealed that the Cabinet Minister Jonathan Aitken had stayed for free at the Ritz Hotel in Paris at the same time as a group of Saudi arms dealers, leading to Aitken's subsequent unsuccessful libel case and imprisonment for perjury.

During this period, from 1988 to February 1998, Al-Fayed's spokesman was Michael Cole, a former BBC journalist, although Cole's PR work for Al-Fayed did not cease in 1998. Hamilton lost a subsequent libel action against Al-Fayed in December 1999 and a subsequent appeal against the verdict in December 2000. The former MP has always denied that he was paid by Al-Fayed for asking questions in parliament. Hamilton's libel action related to a Channel 4 Dispatches documentary broadcast on 16 January 1997 in which Al-Fayed made claims that the MP had received up to £110,000 in cash and received other gratuities for asking parliamentary questions. Hamilton's basis for his appeal was that the original verdict was invalid because Al-Fayed had paid £10,000 for documents stolen from the dustbins of Hamilton's legal representatives by Benjamin Pell.

Diana had been causing problems for the royals as well. Back in 1992, Andrew Morton released a biography in a book about her called *Diana: Her True Story*. Any royal reading it knew she was involved, even though her name wasn't mentioned. But it was obvious that she was collaborating, and she provided information about the inside workings of the royals and her mistreatment by the royals. That really upset the Queen. Others received some very strong letters from Phillip within ten days. Then, in 1995, Diana went on television, and what she had said in the book, she now said on TV. That was more of a very full-on situation than just being an unnamed collaborator of a book.

After that, in December, the Queen sent Diana a letter telling her that she and Charles should get a divorce, and that's what they did in August of 1996. But the Queen took it a lot further than just a divorce. She actually divorced her from the whole royal family and removed her HRH title. Once the Queen had done that, then she was outside of the royal circle.

When Diana had gone to Mohamed Al Fayed's villa, she met his son Dodi, and that's where they struck up a relationship. When the relationship continued after the holiday, that was another thing that the royals didn't like. Her death happened only three days after the conclusion of that holiday.

Q. Why would the French be involved?

A. Why would they support the royal family? They wouldn't. So, why are the French involved? It's because of the landmines. Arms are a huge sector of the French government. That's why they would get on board. The same goes for Tony Blair and Bill Clinton. It's interesting that Bill Clinton made an announcement while Diana was still alive that he was signing an anti-landmine treaty on the 7th of September. After the crash when Diana died, Bill Clinton made another statement saying that they had reversed the decision, and the U.S. would not be signing the treaty.

President Clinton announced that the United States would not sign a treaty supported by nearly 100 other nations to ban the use of anti-personnel land mines. The United States had offered to sign the treaty only if it was amended to allow the continued use of land mines along the tense border between North and South Korea for at least 19 more years and to allow the use of anti-personnel mines in conjunction with anti-tank mines. Mr. Clinton insisted on the exemptions at the urging of the Defense Department, which warned that the United States would invite disaster on the Korean Peninsula if it removed the nearly one million land mines that seed the border between the two Koreas.[9]

Q. At the beginning of the interview, you mentioned Diana's letter thinking that she was going to be killed in a car accident. Who did she suspect was going to kill her?

A. She gave that note that I mentioned earlier to her butler. Also, in the same month, she had a meeting with her lawyer about her divorce. At the end of the meeting, she told her lawyer that she expected to die in an organized car crash. He had actually gone home that night, wrote a note, and locked it in his safe.

So, there were two notes of which she was fearful. In the first note, it actually named her husband, and in 1995, that was Charles. When she talked to the lawyer, there was no name mentioned. But when she spoke with people, she sort of feared that it would be MI6 that would do her in. But basically on the instructions of the senior royals or the establishment.

Listen to the full interview with John Morgan on my website:

https://www.alanrwarren.com/hom-podcast-episodes/episode/5eefe8c1/princess-diana-death-john-morgan-2014

1. CNN.com - "Diana letter 'warned of car plot' - Oct. 20, 2003" http://www.cnn.com/2003/WORLD/europe/10/20/diana.letter/index.html
2. https://en.wikipedia.org/wiki/Mohamed_Al-Fayed
3. Mohamed Al Fayed - Alchetron, The Free Social Encyclopedia. https://alchetron.com/Mohamed-Al-Fayed
4. https://en.wikipedia.org/wiki/Dodi_Fayed
5. Henri Paul | Gyaanipedia Wiki | Fandom. https://gyaanipedia.fandom.com/wiki/Henri_Paul
6. Henri Paul - Alchetron, The Free Social Encyclopedia. https://alchetron.com/Henri-Paul
7. https://en.wikipedia.org/wiki/Trevor_Rees-Jones_(bodyguard)
8. "'Accidents can happen': Warning to Diana from Prince ...." https://www.express.co.uk/news/uk/28297/Accidents-can-happen-Warning-to-Diana-from-Prince-Charles-s-friend
9. "Clinton Still Firmly Against Land-Mine Treaty - The New ...." https://www.nytimes.com/1997/10/11/world/clinton-still-firmly-against-land-mine-treaty.html

Alan Power

INTERVIEW WITH ALAN POWER

In 2014, we decided that we would combine the two shows that I was producing at the time, *The WarrenXchange*, which covered paranormal mysteries, and *The House of Mystery*, which discussed true crime and history. We started running five days a week. I started looking back at past historical events that people continued to talk about no matter how many years had gone by or whatever law enforcement said happened, such as the Kennedy assassination, missing airplanes, and Princess Diana's death.

Of course, after doing the next couple of years of interviews on these subjects, I soon realized that conspiracy theories were a large part of it all. As usual, with any interview, you have to try and look at what the guest is saying from an evidential point of view. How anybody feels about the people involved really isn't enough to convict them of committing the crime.

By 2013, with the surge of self-published books, magazines, and internet blogs, a lot of writers just started saying whatever they thought without any evidence at all. Now, there was one less screening process on written works – the publisher. Publishers used to screen their books and check facts before publishing them, so they would not get sued for publishing misinformation. With the new self-publishing boom, that fact-checking process was now gone. Writers were beginning to publish things based completely on their feelings, and because they believed so much in their theory, they sometimes created evidence. Unfortunately, this started to become a mainstream theme online, and people started to believe the lies. These two authors are a perfect example of this.

Within two months of Alan Power releasing his book on Princess Diana, John Morgan published a book calling Power's book all lies. Power's response was to think that perhaps the MI6 or British establishment was behind Morgan's book.

I interviewed Alan Power one day after John Morgan in 2014. I had no idea about the conflict between the two of them until I talked with them. In such cases, it's easy for an author to blame unidentifiable people as the culprit by naming them as a group such as the CIA or MI6. Anything that happens to them after they publish their book can be therefore blamed on the same group, making the author look like they are not only a true patriot by exposing the truth, but they are in danger for doing so.

Here is the bio that Alan Power sent to us for the show:

"Author Alan Power is married to Sally and has enjoyed a variety of interests, including being a drama student, an official candidate of the Conservative party, and owning his own company, but this is his first journey into the world of writing.

He has written another book about Diana that will be published later and has ideas for other *subjects that will also follow. When his company suffered the ravages of internal fraud with no joy from the police due to lack of evidence and a degree of police indifference, his life changed irrevocably, but now he had the time to write.*

When Diana was murdered, Alan remembers feeling rage that such a beautiful and natural person as Diana could be used, abused, and so cruelly discarded just to serve the monarchy's needs. He considered the probability that this was a murder of convenience and monarchical survival, so he began an extensive investigation into Diana's death.

Although initially unsure he would be up to this task, he persevered and now offers evidence that this murder was not conducted by rogue MI6 officers, considered as possible during the inquests, but by serving MI6 officers and with the use of military aid.

This project began in 2003, and despite many attempts by others to prevent or delay the book's release, Alan now brings you his findings. There is first an overview of the background to this brutal act and a selection of relevant events prior to the inquests, with lateral thought being applied to four million words of cross-referenced inquest evidence. He delivers the most compelling and damming evidence and says that it's important for justice to prevail if Britain still wishes to be considered a democracy."[1]

Q. What got you to write about this case?

A. One thing that really annoys me intensely was the state of the British nation and the monarchy, and the fact that they were treating Diana Spencer and then the issue when she was murdered. I was so enraged by it I thought something had to be done about it. Then, I thought, what can I do about it? Then, I thought if everyone said that, nothing would ever happen, so I gave it a go. I started it in November of 2003, and I just went flat out researching details, interviewing people, and by 2006, I had written the nonfiction side of it. It's a strange mix. The first half of the book is nonfiction, and the second is a story from, in my view, what happened.

Then, in 2007, the inquest was coming out. So, I had to spend a lot more time researching that to add to the evidence I already had. It gave me a chance to assess what happened during the inquest, what I knew had happened before, and the issues or the points that they hadn't brought out at the inquest. Also, the main points that they ignored, which gave me a lot more clout to write my book.

Q. How was it researching a case like Diana's death? How were people's responses to you while investigating?

A. By in large, very well. Most of the witnesses didn't like what happened any more than I did. But it was a very difficult position because they witnessed events take place, and they obviously had some pressure on them not to respond in too cold of a way. I think it's fair to say this. I had one, for example, the Japanese confidentially doing some work. And I was fairly sure I could get some of these witnesses to come along and talk to us, get on camera, and be on Japanese television. But I couldn't get one single witness to take part.

Q. Why is that? What was the fear behind it?

A. Basically, I think it was intimidation on the part of the British police and indeed the French. They were just controlling the whole thing. They clamped down on the whole thing. It was not to be released what happened or who had been responsible for her death. They intimidated people. I have been intimidated myself. They try to intimidate people from taking a risk. It didn't work on me, but it has worked on a lot of other people.

Q. How do you think the plan came about to kill Princess Diana?

A. My personal view is, it's pretty clear to me that the nod came from the palace to MI6 to continue with the assassination.

Q. Why do you think that Diana had to be killed?

A. There are a lot of reasons that people have come up with. Such as the landmine situation and being a nuisance all throughout the world. In the arms industry, and the cash that they were making from the arms industry. Perhaps there's some truth in that. But the main central reason that the monarchy was involved was that Diana had been abused since the beginning. Charles was even shacking up with Camilla Parker Bowles. She was just used for one particular purpose. She knew that. Obviously, not at the time. But later on, she did.

Camilla Parker Bowles, Duchess of Cornwall, is a member of the British royal family. She received her title upon her marriage to Charles, Prince of Wales, heir apparent to the British throne, on 9 April 2005. It is a second marriage for both of them. Despite being entitled to be known as Princess of Wales, she uses the title Duchess of Cornwall, her husband's secondary designation.

In Scotland, she is known as the Duchess of Rothesay. Camilla was periodically romantically involved with the Prince of Wales both before and during their first marriages. The relationship became highly publicized in the media and attracted worldwide scrutiny.[2]

Once Harry was born, that was it. Her job was done. She said that when Harry was born, Charles was at the hospital with her. And as soon as he was born, he left. She knew at that moment he had gone to be with his baby. That was it. It was over. He had done his job, his duty, and the children were there.

Then, of course, she got very annoyed by it. And she was very independent, a very strong individual, and she wasn't going to put up with it. She had lots of evidence about what they had been getting up to at the palace. All of the "sexploits."

She made up a thick dossier on this. She had two copies of it. She gave one copy to her friend Simone Simons. Simone got nervous, unfortunately, and said she destroyed it after it being under her mattress for about one month. She was very nervous about what was going on behind the scenes and after Diana was murdered.

Simone Simmons, a healer by profession, formed a friendship with Diana. They met almost every day and spent several hours on the telephone. Diana told Simone she wanted her to write a book that revealed the truth about her. Simone wrote the book *Diana: The Last Word,* about her time counseling the princess.

Princess Diana's psychic has revealed the tragic royal's final secrets and released never-before-heard answerphone messages she left before her untimely death 23 years ago. According to Simone, Diana

- Was preparing to name and shame a mob of dangerous international arms dealers the morning of her untimely death,
- Wanted to move to America like Meghan Markle to escape the limelight and

wanted to buy actress Julie Andrews' home in LA,
- Wasn't in love with her Dodi Fayed when she died and was instead intent on reuniting with her heart surgeon lover Hasnat Khan,
- Opened up to her about her deepest sex secrets – including her hatred of making love to men with hairy backs,
- Recruited ex-rugby player Will Carling to give her a personal training program that would get rid of her bulimia-ravaged body and give her curves.³

So, I think that was the prime reason for it. Also, the police then sometimes tried to track down this dossier by searching all of the homes.

Q. Was the driver Henri Paul involved?

A. No. Henri Paul was basically conned into running the show. He was basically a very loyal servant and employee of the Ritz Hotel under Dodi. He did his job looking after them, driving them around occasionally just to help out. No, he certainly wasn't involved, and he was known to have been cooperative. He was ex-military, and he was used to doing what he was told.

He was structured by MI6 to set the whole thing in motion – to be where they wanted to be, and use the car they chose. They chose the particular car without tinted windows. They got him to drive it instead of using their daily chauffeur. They knew he would drive and instructed him to take that particular route. They had to enter the tunnel. Otherwise, there would have been no assassination.

But I think that Henri Paul was also a target because he would know what they were telling him to do and who was telling him to do it. If he survived, then he could give some pretty serious evidence against them.

The Secret Intelligence Service, commonly known as "MI6," is the foreign intelligence service of the

United Kingdom, tasked mainly with the covert overseas collection and analysis of human intelligence in support of the UK's national security. Formed in 1909 as a section of the Secret Service Bureau specializing in foreign intelligence, the section experienced dramatic growth during World War I and officially adopted its current name around 1920.

The name "MI6," meaning Military Intelligence, Section 6, originated as a flag of convenience during World War II when SIS was known by many names. It is still commonly used today.

The stated priority roles of MI6 are counterterrorism, counter-proliferation, providing intelligence in support of cybersecurity, and supporting stability overseas to disrupt terrorism and other criminal activities. Unlike its main sister agencies, the Security Service, known as "MI5," and Government Communications Headquarters, known as "GCH," MI6 works exclusively in foreign intelligence gathering and allows it to carry out operations only against persons outside the British Islands.[4]

Q. Dodi Fayed, did they want him dead as well?

A. No. I think the number one target was Diana. She had got to go. I think the fact that he was in the car was, in fact, a bonus, and they could get the whole lot wiped out at once. I think the only one that wasn't really a target was Trevor Rees-Jones.

Q. What are your thoughts on the ambulance and doctors not attending to Diana properly?

A. There are a lot of situations where you can discuss that sort of thing. But the problem is what I've got, and all good investigators have, is that we can only put down the facts. All it is that we can prove and not stuff that you believe might be the case. So, when it came to the ambulance, frankly, there is no evidence. There are documents of who said what and who they said it to. But there is nothing really definitive, and you can draw conclusions. If you want to put down opinions as facts to make a story, then I guess you can. I'm not prepared to do that. That's not investigative.

Listen to the full interview with Alan Power on my website:

www.alanrwarren.com/hom-podcast-episodes/episode/733d763e/alan-power-princess-diana-death-2014

---

1. https://www.facebook.com/AlanPowerAuthor
2. https://en.wikipedia.org/wiki/Camilla,_Duchess_of_Cornwall
3. "Princess Diana pal shares haunting unheard messages and …." https://www.dailystar.co.uk/news/latest-news/princess-diana-pal-shares-haunting-22670578
4. https://en.wikipedia.org/wiki/Secret_Intelligence_Service

References

All interviews were taken from the the *House of Mystery Radio Show* between 2010 and 2020. The show airs on several radio stations throughout the United States, including

- KKNW 1150 A.M. in Seattle/Tacoma,
- KCAA 106.5 F.M. in Los Angeles,
- KCAA 102.3 F.M. Riverside,
- KCAA 1050 A.M. Palm Springs,
- KFNX 1100 A.M. Phoenix,
- KFNX 540 A.M. Salt Lake City,
- on my website: alanrwarren.com/house-of-mystery-radioshow

Below is a list of our guests and their works in reference to the mysterious celebrity deaths:

1. Alan Power: *Exposed: The Princess Diana Conspiracy - Revised Edition: The Evidence of Murder*, ASIN: B00JG2GDK4, Probity Press Ltd, April 2, 2014.
2. John Morgan: *How They Murdered Princess*

Diana: The Shocking Truth, ASIN: B00R6WH4P4, December 17, 2014.
3. Marti Rulli: *Goodbye Natalie, Goodbye Splendour*, ASIN: B00J90C1BS, Open Road Media, April 1, 2014.
4. John Hook: *Who Killed Bob Crane?: The Final Close-Up*, ISBN-10: 1944194258, ISBN-13: 978-1944194253, Get Hooked Media, February 21, 2017.
5. Robert Crane: *Crane: Sex, Celebrity, and My Father's Unsolved Murder* (Screen Classics), ASIN: B00UIK74OM, The University Press of Kentucky, March 10, 2015.
6. Paul Davids: *Marilyn Monroe Declassified*, ASIN: B01LBIHPCU, September 27, 2016.
7. Matthew Richer, Tom Grant: *The Mysterious Death of Kurt Cobain: Suicide or Murder? You Decide*, ASIN: B01E07YUCM, April 7, 2016.
8. Benjamin Statler, Director: *Soaked In Bleach*, ASIN: B00YAZNBTI, August 14, 2015.

About Alan R. Warren

Alan R. Warren has written several bestselling True Crime books and has been one of the hosts and producers of the popular NBC news talk radio show the *House of Mystery*, which reviews True Crime, History, Science, Religion, Paranormal mysteries that we live with every day. From a darker, comedic, and logical perspective, he has interviewed guests such as Robert Kennedy Jr., F. Lee Bailey, Aphrodite Jones, Marcia Clark, Nancy Grace, Dan Abrams, and Jesse Ventura. The show is based in Seattle on KKNW 1150 AM and syndicated on the NBC network throughout the United States, including on KCAA 106.5 FM Los

Angeles/Riverside/Palm Springs, as well in Utah, New Mexico, and Arizona.

Read more about Alan on his website: *www.alanrwarren.com*

About Eric Shapiro

Eric Shapiro is a writer and filmmaker. Called "the next Philip K. Dick" by author Kealan Patrick Burke, Shapiro is the author of six critically acclaimed fiction books, among them the novella *It's Only Temporary* (2005), which appeared on *Nightmare Magazine's* list of the Top 100 Horror Books, and numerous short stories published in anthologies alongside work by H.P. Lovecraft, Ray Bradbury, Stephen King, Chuck Palahniuk, and many others. His nonfiction articles have been published on *The Daily Dot*, *Ravishly*, and *The Good Men Project*. His first feature film, *Rule of 3* (2010), won awards at the Fantasia International Film Festival and Shriekfest, and had its U.S. premiere at Fantastic Fest. His second feature film, *Living*

Things (2014), was endorsed by PETA (People for the Ethical Treatment of Animals) and distributed by Cinema Libre Studio. In 2015, he won the 19th Annual Fade In Award for Thriller Screenplays. He was a founding partner of Ghostwriters Central, a writing and editing firm which has received positive notices from *The Wall Street Journal*, *Consumers Digest*, and the TV program *Intelligence For Your Life*. Eric has edited works published on *The Huffington Post* and *Forbes*, as well as two Bram Stoker Award-nominated novels. He lives in Northern California with his wife, Rhoda, and their two sons.

Also in the House of Mystery Radio Show Interview Series

The *House of Mystery Radio Show* has been on the air for ten years, broadcasting in over a dozen cities in the U.S. It started as a way to interview guests knowledgeable in many of the world's mysteries involving crime, science, religion, history, paranormal, conspiracies, etc. The House of Mystery Interview series is a curated collection of interviews from the show. Each volume focuses on one of the mysteries, providing the background and reproducing the main points discussed in the interviews. There will be no committed answer at the end, as the Interviews series does not attempt to solve the case. Instead, it provides the most compelling aspects of each theory held by different experts. This series is an excellent reference for researchers and a good overview for those unfamiliar with the case. Online links to the actual interviews are included.

VOLUME 1: JACK THE RIPPER: THE INTERVIEWS

Volume 1 of the Interview Series, "Jack the Ripper," covers the ultimate "who-done-it" mystery of 1888 London. Scotland Yard's "Whitechapel Murder File," in which Jack the Ripper had a starring role, went cold before it could be solved. One hundred thirty-two years later, and the fascination with this cold case mystery continues. Ripperologists passionately debate suspects, opinions, research methods, and theories. Even which murder victims to include in the case is widely debated. Astonishingly, work continues, and today Ripperologists still find new clues that bring us closer to solving the mystery.

The mix of credible and diverse thinkers interviewed includes world-renowned historian Neil Storey, the Godfather of Ripper Research, Paul Begg, Ripperologists: Paul Williams, Tom Wescott, Adam Wood, and Steve Blomer. Michael Hawley contributes his unprecedented scientific approach to the case. Suspect Ripperologists Jeff Mudgett, whose great-great-grandfather was serial killer H.H. Holmes, weighs in, as does Russell Edwards, who believes he solved the mystery through DNA.

VOLUME 2: JFK ASSASSINATION: THE INTERVIEWS

Volume 2 of the Interview Series, "JFK Assassination," covers *the* unrivaled historical mystery of historical mysteries. The JFK assassination is the grandfather of all conspiracies in America and arguably where they all started. A highly popular President with movie star looks and charisma, effecting significant changes in society, was brutally cut down in his prime. The official story was that JFK was killed by a sole assassin, Lee Harvey Oswald. However, many conspiracy theorists believe in an assassination plot involving the FBI, CIA, U.S. military, VP LBJ, Cuba's Fidel Castro, Russia's KGB, the Mafia, or some combination of those entities.

The research and interviewing of the JFK assassination experts lasted for over six years. Arguments and counter-arguments from a diverse mix of bestselling authors make for some interesting discussions. And some of the authors interviewed are considered just as controversial as the mystery itself. Most authors focused on who they believe was responsible for the assassination. Others narrowed their focus on certain related aspects, such as the Zapruder film, Nix film, Garrison Tapes, etc. All information collected from each expert adds value to the overall mystery.

VOLUME 3: ZODIAC KILLER: THE INTERVIEWS

Volume 3 of the Interview Series, "Zodiac Killer," covers another serial killer who has stayed in the spotlight for years after their case has gone cold. It's been over 40 years now, and fascination with the Zodiac is still going strong. Experts passionately debate Zodiac suspects, Zodiac's letters/ciphers, opinions, and theories. Even which murder victims to include in the case is widely debated.

The diverse mix of authors interviewed includes cryptologist and cipher expert David Oranchak, authors who propose their suspects are already convicted serial killers, authors who claim the Zodiac was their father, authors who offer new or already considered suspects, and an author who argues the Zodiac killer didn't exist at all and that Zodiac was a hoax.

www.ingramcontent.com/pod-product-compliance
Lightning Source LLC
Chambersburg PA
CBHW071426070526
44578CB00001B/17